# Britain's Unsolved Murders

# Britain's Unsolved Murders

*By*

**Kevin Turton**

PEN & SWORD
TRUE CRIME

First published in Great Britain in 2019 by
Pen & Sword True Crime
An imprint of
Pen & Sword Books Ltd
Yorkshire - Philadelphia

ISBN 978 1 52672 632 2

A CIP catalogue record for this book is
available from the British Library.

Printed and bound in England
By TJ International Ltd.

Pen & Sword Books Ltd incorporates the Imprints of Pen & Sword Books
Archaeology, Atlas, Aviation, Battleground, Discovery, Family History, History,
Maritime, Military, Naval, Politics, Railways, Select, Transport, True Crime,
Fiction, Frontline Books, Leo Cooper, Praetorian Press, Seaforth Publishing,
Wharncliffe and White Owl.

For a complete list of Pen & Sword titles please contact

PEN & SWORD BOOKS LIMITED
47 Church Street, Barnsley, South Yorkshire, S70 2AS, England
E-mail: enquiries@pen-and-sword.co.uk
Website: www.pen-and-sword.co.uk

or

PEN AND SWORD BOOKS
1950 Lawrence Rd, Havertown, PA 19083, USA
E-mail: uspen-and-sword@casematepublishers.com
Website: www.penandswordbooks.com

# Contents

# Acknowledgements

I would like to thank all the authors listed below whose works have aided my research, along with various institutions and of course my partner, Maureen Yule, who has given me her unstinting support in putting this book together.

Northampton Central Library

Ipswich Public Records Office

*The Encyclopedia of Forensic Science* by Brian Lane

*Silent Witnesses* by Nigel McCreery

*The Peasenhall Murder* by Martin Fido & Keith Skinner

*The Camden Town Murder* by David Barrat

*The Trial of Harold Greenwood* by Winifred Duke

*Death at Wolf's Nick* by Diane Janes

The *Daily Mail*

The *Leeds Mercury*

The National Newspaper Archive

Bradford Libraries

Scotland's National Archives

# Introduction

When Edgar Allan Poe invented Detective Auguste Dupin, he created a genre that some 170 or so years later would dominate the visual, audio and literary marketplace, namely that of crime fiction. Seized upon by writers like Emile Gaboriau in France, James M'Govan in Scotland and London writer Mary Braddon, it began its steady rise to the top end of mainstream fiction throughout the nineteenth century. Wilkie Collins, Charles Dickens, Arthur Morrison and America's Nick Carter, alongside various others, added to the list of writers who realized crime sold books and used it in various fictional formats.

For those with limited reading skills, and that would have included much of the population throughout the first half of the nineteenth century, publishers sought to develop highly illustrated magazines alongside their stories. This, in turn, gave birth to the 'Penny Bloods'. These were well-illustrated, poorly written, sensational accounts of mayhem and murder. The more bloodshed the better. Sold to an unsophisticated public, their intent was simply to make money. So initially the stories told were pure fiction, but by around 1850 this had begun to change. Publishers realized that fiction and fact could be woven together to produce stories that were perhaps more realistic; this in turn gave birth to the serial, which allowed long-running stories to develop centred around real events.

When the Education of Act of 1880 arrived, ensuring every child had an education, the reading public had already begun to become more discerning. They wanted to understand more about the criminal mind. Sensationalism was no longer seen as being the most effective way to sell a story. The reading audience slowly widened and, through better education, became more sophisticated. Newspapers, ever aware of their readership, saw the change and seized upon it. They realized murder trials sold more copies, so these were more closely followed and reported in far greater detail than at any point in the past. In turn, that led to a major change in the world of crime fiction. The 'Penny Bloods' faded into memory and the erudite, puzzle-solving detective was born. It was the era of Sherlock Holmes, improved policing and the birth of forensic science.

Sir Arthur Conan Doyle clearly led the way, basing his character Sherlock Holmes on Edinburgh surgeon Dr Joseph Bell. He developed a criminal investigator with a curious eye and a forensic mind; a thinking man's detective who had a fascination for all things criminal and a perplexing ability to interpret crime scenes in a way readers had never believed possible. Others followed: author R Austin Freeman created scientific detective Dr John Thorndyke; Baroness Orczy was one of the first armchair detectives; then there was Ernest Bramah's blind detective Max Carrados and, of course, G.K. Chesterton's Father Brown. Many more joined the list and, in various ways, through their fictional crime-solving techniques came the growth in a new genre, that of true crime.

By the dawn of the twentieth century, the belief that a criminal will always carry away some trace from the scene of a crime and leave behind a trace of their own presence had been born. So too had the realization that police are not always best placed to solve crime. Fiction writers turned more toward the private-eye. Raymond Chandler developed the eponymous Philip Marlowe, Erle Stanley Gardner gave us the unbeatable American lawyer Perry Mason, Chester Gould invented the Dick Tracy character and H.C. McNeile brought out Bulldog Drummond, to name but a few. Crime had essentially become an area of study where the reader was to be confounded by the perplexity of the crime, with the solution only to be found by the hero.

Agatha Christie took that idea to a whole new level with Poirot and the quiet village sleuth, Miss Marple. Then television took hold of the whole crime genre and visualized the written plot, and along came the TV detective, followed by a plethora of true crime from around the world. But as we know all too well, even though these enigmatic, often flawed characters seem infallible, the plain and simple truth is that not every crime is solved. Our heroes may crack every crime they meet, but for police forces up and down the country, murder is at times the most difficult crime to resolve.

Over the last 150 years, many of these so-called unsolvable murder cases have become the subject of books, films and docu-dramas, occasionally resurrected by local newspapers and re-examined on their anniversary, or their details reassembled to try to ascertain if modern forensic methods can make any impact. Generally, nothing new is ever found unless the case is within the last twenty or thirty years. But that is not to say we should leave these on the 'unsolved' pile. The victims of murder, regardless of time past, still deserve justice. I believe their voices should still be heard, and so I have selected a number of murder cases that over the years have both confounded and frustrated police and the law courts. Some are complex, others simply enigmatic, but for the families of the victims they remain forever unsolved.

## Chapter 1

# The Poisoning of Emile L'Angelier

*The Madeleine Smith mystery, 1857*

French-speaking Pierre Emile L'Angelier – Emile to those who knew him – was born in 1823 in the predominantly English-speaking Channel Island town of Jersey and spent the first eighteen years of his life living between the French coast and the British mainland. Like much of the Channel Islands at this time, an influx of British soldiers, brought in during and after the Napoleonic Wars, had changed the island's culture and language. Many had chosen to settle in the islands at the wars' end, while others decided to return at the end of their military service. As a result, Jersey had begun to develop as an agricultural exporter; something the L'Angelier family would have recognized and no doubt embraced, particularly as his father was employed as a nurseryman. But it seems that for Emile, whatever the personal career prospects offered by those burgeoning markets, his future lay elsewhere.

He took ship and left for Scotland in 1841, ostensibly to take up a position on a private estate in Dundee where he was to learn the skills of estate management. But it seems the death of the estate owner a few months after his arrival forced a change of plan and direction. By late the following year he was in Edinburgh working for a seed merchant, perhaps an initial drop down the employed ranks. However, he persevered, learned new skills and remained there for some three-and-a-half years.

My belief is that during this time he also embarked upon his first serious love affair. The woman concerned, only ever referred to as 'the Lady from Fife', was to have an enduring impact on the rest of his life. When it came to an inevitable end, she being of a higher status in society than he could have ever attained, he made plans to leave the city. He was back in Jersey by late spring 1846 and in France toward the end of that year. There he stayed for a number of years, joined the National Guard in Paris at some point in 1847 and played a part in the 'June Days Uprising' in Paris during the 1848 revolution.

The start of 1851 found him back in Edinburgh but in straitened circumstances, struggling for work and, without any financial means, needing a place to stay. A chance encounter with an old acquaintance from Jersey whom he had met five years earlier proved manna from heaven. Robert Baker, a waiter for his landlord uncle at the city's Rainbow Tavern, offered a free bed. L'Angelier was in no position to refuse. It became his place of refuge and there he stayed for some nine months. It was a difficult period of his life. He was depressed, if his friend was to be believed, at times almost suicidal and obsessed with the love affair that had gone so wrong. Emile L'Angelier was in a bad place. It took until January of the following year to turn things around.

He moved out of the tavern at the end of that month and made his way to Dundee, where he took a job paying eight shillings (40p) a week with free board and lodgings working alongside nurseryman William Pringle. The financial side of his life had been resolved. But the past, like a festering wound, still irritated, and an embittered L'Angelier was all too ready to unburden himself to any who would listen. News of his affair in Fife had become common knowledge by mid-summer. So had his behaviour, which at times was disturbing, with threats of suicide, angry outbursts and wide mood swings being noticed more and more. There was even talk of his use and knowledge of arsenic, something that would eventually play a major part in his life. How much all of this affected his work is not known, but it must have had some impact because by late July 1852, he had left Dundee and begun a new life in Glasgow.

Scotland's largest city at this time, Glasgow's population was in excess of 300,000, with a large proportion Irish-born. The arrival of shipyards like Tod & MacGregor in Partick and Napiers in Govan, industrial expansion north of the Forth and the growth of the railways had brought wealth and skilled employment. For L'Angelier, it obviously offered more opportunity for advancement than Dundee. He took a job working at Huggins & Co., Commission Agents (essentially middlemen), on Bothwell Street, lodged nearby with Elizabeth Wallace and her family and set about carving out a better work and social life in what he perceived to be a vibrant new city. The Fife affair had been left behind and was no longer discussed. He became a regular in the Sunday congregation at nearby St Jude's Church, built a number of friendships and proved himself to be a worthwhile addition to the Huggins workforce. Gone was the melancholia that had dogged him in Dundee, and in its place he found a renewed lust for life.

Early in 1854, and keen to improve his station in life even more, L'Angelier changed his lodging and moved in with Peter Clark, curator of the Royal Botanic Garden, and his wife. He had a higher status and better prospects. As a result, health, work, temperament and social standing all improved. So too did his finances. Working at Huggins had significantly increased his weekly income, which of course brought benefits, and by the start of 1855 he was probably feeling more secure than at any time in his life. All that was needed to complete the picture was a new woman on his arm, and he knew just who he wanted that to be.

Through his regular attendance at church he had met and formed a strong friendship with spinster Mary Perry. Throughout the latter part of 1854 and the early winter months of 1855, the friendship blossomed, though not as a love affair. She became his confidante. The two met regularly at her home on Renfrew Street, often dining together. When meeting was difficult or perhaps not possible, they wrote letters to each other. For L'Angelier, she became, over the period of a few months, perhaps the most important and certainly closest friend in his fast-changing world. So when he first saw near-neighbour Madeleine Smith, it was Mary whom he first approached for information. I have no doubt they discussed his attraction to Madeleine at length. But Madeleine Smith was never going to be easy to meet. Convention demanded a formal introduction, and Mary was not best placed to organize such a thing. He turned instead to brothers Charles and Robert Baird, both acquainted with L'Angelier through his work and both well-known in the social circles that mattered in Glasgow because of their late father, prominent Scottish writer Robert Baird. Charles proved unhelpful, but Robert thought he could bring the two together through his uncle or, failing that, his mother. He was thwarted on both counts. Polite society in the 1850s was obviously not so easily circumvented. His introduction to her was eventually left to a contrived, clumsy meeting on the street. Perhaps not the best of beginnings, but it seemed to work and by April 1855, the two were corresponding with each other regularly. The love affair was up and running.

But this was never likely to be as successful as L'Angelier may have imagined. The Smiths were a wealthy, upper middle-class family of seven at this time, their daily lives governed by the social mores of the period and aided by in-house servants. L'Angelier, on the other hand, had little status and even less wealth. It is debatable whether he knew at the time how well regarded the family was amongst the affluent, moneyed class of established

Glasgow society. It certainly never stopped him in his relentless pursuit of the Smiths' eldest daughter, though at this early stage the relationship was clandestine, Madeleine all too well aware of how her father, James, would have reacted had he known of their meeting. Highly respected and exceptionally well thought of, James Smith was one of Scotland's most widely admired architects. Born in Alloa in 1808, he followed his own father to Glasgow in 1826. A few years later he collaborated with David and James Hamilton (two renowned architects) on the design of the Royal Exchange Square and The Royal Bank of Scotland, and eventually married David Hamilton's daughter, Janet. Between 1840 and the time of L'Angelier's arrival on the scene in 1855, he had also designed the Victoria Baths, the Collegiate School at Garnet Hill and was about to begin work on the McLellan Galleries on Sauchiehall Street, not to mention other key design projects he had been involved with. He also owned two homes: one on Glasgow's India Street, where the family spent the winter, and another, 'Rowaleyn', on the Gairloch near Helensburgh, the family's summer home. Their's was clearly a family name to be aware of amongst Glasgow's elite, and one L'Angelier grew ever more familiar with as time passed.

Madeleine's caution regarding their relationship was a constant reminder to L'Angelier of just how difficult it was likely to be to break into the Smith family in any serious way. Although it never put him off, it certainly tempered their meetings, which were usually kept short and always away from public gaze. In order to maintain contact and keep knowledge of her association with L'Angelier secret from her family, they wrote letters to each other on an almost daily basis. Trusted house servant Christina Haggart was used by Madeleine as the go-between. To keep all this correspondence away from her family, Madeleine had L'Angelier address his letters to the servant, or occasionally use an alias, Miss Bruce. Haggart would then pass them on. The system worked well for a while, but eventually a house servant receiving mail on a regular basis aroused suspicion and Madeleine decided to end the relationship. It was a half-hearted attempt, which made little impact on L'Angelier, and before the family went off to 'Rowaleyn' for summer they were back in touch, meeting whenever possible at the house in India Street. Haggart ensured she opened the gate at the back of the house to allow him access to the laundry room where Madeleine waited. If meetings proved difficult, they would leave letters by the garden gate.

Early that same summer (1855), swept along by his belief that their shared passion was genuine and enduring, L'Angelier asked Madeleine to marry him. She readily agreed. So in August, considering himself engaged, he arranged secretly for her to meet his great friend Mary Perry. The meeting was a success and within weeks Madeleine was corresponding with her, comfortable in the knowledge that Mary would keep their secret. But really it was all too fanciful. Marriage to Emile L'Angelier could never have held any real prospect of success, and Madeleine must have known that. Obtaining her father's approval for the match, which she knew was of paramount importance, was beyond countenance. If they were to marry they must elope and do so secretly. It was the stuff of novels – romantic, idealistic and impractical – and Madeleine must have also known that. But they both revelled in the idea of being a married couple, Madeleine beginning to address her letters to 'My own beloved husband' or 'My own darling husband' and signing herself 'Mimi', a pet name given her by L'Angelier. All the time she maintained secrecy from all those she knew, with the exception of her servant and Mary Perry.

But that summer also brought its own problems. Because Madeleine followed her family out to 'Rowaleyn', it became difficult that first year to arrange any further meeting away from her parents. There followed a long-enforced absence, during which the relationship could only be conducted by letter. L'Angelier, unhappy at the separation, and perhaps by late summer somewhat disillusioned, suddenly threatened to end the affair and move to Lima in Peru, a city whose fortunes had improved significantly at this time through the export of guano (excrement from seabirds), which European countries were buying, having identified it as an extremely effective fertilizer. It was probably no more than a hollow threat, but enough to prompt Madeleine to write to him in September 1855, saying: 'It will break my heart if you go away. You know not how I love you, Emile. I live for you alone; I adore you.'

Reassured, he stayed in Scotland and by winter, with the Smiths back on India Street, their secret meetings were once again a more regular occurrence, though not always without incident and often with L'Angelier being the cause. At the end of November he was taken ill. Madeleine wrote to him on 3 December, urging him to seek medical advice and help. The illness, though not defined, is one she had become aware of some weeks earlier and she showed genuine concern: 'I think you should consult Dr M'Farlane; that is go and see him. Get him to sound you – tell you what is wrong with you.'

Whether or not he ever took the advice is not known, but on Christmas Day that same year, after dining with Glasgow merchant William Roberts he was again taken ill. According to the merchant, after sharing the same meal as all his other guests, L'Angelier was taken violently ill, vomiting and purging for over two hours before he could be taken back to his lodgings. These were symptoms that would show themselves time and again in the future.

Whether Madeleine was ever aware of this incident is not known. She had other things to contend with. By the end of 1855, her mother had again become suspicious of the frequent letters, though not of the man sending them. This forced servant Christina Haggart to be more circumspect and for a time to stop acting as go-between. Correspondence became difficult and less frequent, but by late April 1856, with the family back at 'Rowaleyn', it had become much easier to smuggle letters in and out. It had also become much easier for L'Angelier to gain access to the house and grounds. Throughout the late spring and into summer he made frequent visits, the couple meeting generally at night either by the gated entrance to the house or outside one of the windows. Each meeting was followed by long, often passionate letters from Madeleine, detailing their intimacy. Clearly the affair appears by this time to have become sexual: 'Our intimacy has not been criminal, as I am your wife before God – so it has been no sin our loving each other. No; darling, fond Emile, I am your wife.'

But despite these declarations, the relationship remained difficult. L'Angelier still wanted to marry. He encouraged her to tell her parents, but she resisted. He raised the notion of elopement again and suggested they run away together in September when the family were back in Glasgow. He felt they should let her parents discover the marriage when it was too late to stop, and initially she agreed; September probably seemed a long way off. But as the month drew nearer, she got cold feet and began to play down the idea. Marrying L'Angelier then, as it had been since the start of their relationship, was simply never going to be feasible.

The month came and went without any further discussion. Disappointed, but still believing their strange affair would continue, L'Angelier was reassured by Madeleine's reasoned argument that the timing of their elopement would be better the following year. However, by November 1856 that was looking increasingly unlikely as their infrequent meetings became ever more difficult to maintain.

Back in July that year, L'Angelier had moved to new lodgings at 11 Franklin Place to better facilitate both his work and love life. However, at the end of October James Smith, unaware of his daughter's burgeoning love affair, moved his family from India Street to a new house at 7 Blythswood Square. This added to L'Angelier's difficulty of moving easily between his lodgings and Madeleines' home. It also made gaining access to the new house, at times, impossible: four terraces forming a square facing onto a central garden made him far more visible on the street and severely restricted his ability to get inside unseen, even with the help of a house servant. The erstwhile Christina Haggart was all too willing and remained loyal, but being under Madeleine's mother's watchful eye, she could not so easily smuggle in letters from the Frenchman. Between them, they conjured up a plan that would keep all their correspondence away from prying eyes. He would deliver his letters at night to her window, which was barred and faced the road. These would be left on the sill for Madeleine to retrieve. She would write as normal and Christina would smuggle her letters out of the house and post them on. Meeting face to face could now only happen if her father was away on business. Living arrangements in the new house meant Madeleine shared her bed with sister Janet, but when her father was away Janet moved into her mother's bed for the night; Madeleine could then either see L'Angelier at the window (he would tap it with his cane) or sneak him into the house.

The arrangement worked reasonably well, but events in Madeleine Smith's life were changing. By the start of winter 1856, William Minnoch, a partner in a Glasgow firm of merchants and a friend of the family, became a more regular visitor to the house. He was a favourite of her father and had known the Smiths for four years. Back then, Madeleine had been only 15 years old and hardly ever seen. She was now a vivacious and perceptive young woman. Minnoch was attracted to her, and the two began to meet. He accompanied her to concerts and to the opera. Local gossip followed, and inevitably L'Angelier was told. He wrote to her demanding answers, but she denied any involvement: 'Emile he is P's [father's] friend, and I know he will have him at the house; but need you mind that when I have told you I have no regard for him?'

Of course, she lied: William Minnoch was becoming a very important part of her life. He represented a future that L'Angelier could never provide. No doubt he was all too well aware of that, and never believed Madeleine's constant denials. There was probably also an element of jealousy. He stopped writing. Throughout January 1857 he made no attempt to keep the relationship alive, and at the start of February her letters were turned away unopened.

The affair had cooled. Clearly, for Madeleine that left her with a problem. On 28 January that year, William Minnoch had proposed marriage and she had accepted. But Minnoch did not know about L'Angelier, and the

Frenchman had all of Madeleine's letters in his possession. If she was to avoid scandal of the worst kind, she had to have those letters returned. She wrote to L'Angelier, expressing her anger at having her last letter returned and breaking off their engagement: 'You have more than once returned me my letters, and my mind was made up that I should not stand the same thing again … we had better for the future consider ourselves strangers. I trust to your honour as a gentleman that you will not reveal anything that may have passed between us.'

She went on at length to apprise him of her change of heart, how she had once loved him, wanted to marry him, but how all that had now changed and her love for him had ceased. More importantly, as a consequence of all this, all the letters she had written to him she wanted back. L'Angelier was to bring them to the rear of the house and hand them over to Christina Haggart. In return, twenty-four hours later she would post back to him his own letters. To Madeleine's mind it was the gentlemanly thing to do. Unfortunately for her, L'Angelier was no gentleman.

He read the letter, and his response was immediate: a bitter and spiteful reply informing her that she would never see her letters. Instead, they would be forwarded to her father. He knew just what that would mean. Shame, both public and private, would follow. It would also destroy any future with William Minnoch. Madeleine was devastated. In a powerful, heartfelt plea in response to his threat, she begged him to recant, citing how such a humiliation would destroy the fabric of her own family. Exposing her, she argued, would do irreparable, unwarranted damage to her reputation and force her out of her own home. She ended her letter by asking L'Angelier to come to Blythswood Square the following night (Wednesday, 12 February) at midnight and she would let him into the house.

Whether he did is not known, but the letters stayed with L'Angelier, quite possibly because he was too ill to do much else. At some point later that same week, his landlady, Ann Duthie, had found him in bed at around eight o'clock in the morning complaining of cold and thirst. He had vomited a thick, greenish liquid, which she removed and disposed of. According to L'Angelier, he had been out the previous evening and was seized by pain as he returned.

Following this bout of illness, Madeleine softened her attitude and began to write in more affectionate tones. The love affair was back on. She had perhaps realized that if she was to get her hands on those letters she needed to repair the rift between the two of them. Certainly, L'Angelier was receptive, though of course he still had not heard about her intended marriage to William Minnoch and Madeleine had every intention of keeping it that way. To her mind she was being duplicitous, but with good reason.

On 23 February, he was struck down again with symptoms as before. This time fellow lodger Amadee Thuau went to fetch a doctor, who diagnosed an undefined bilious complaint and prescribed an aperient draught to settle his stomach and then visited him daily for the next three days. Through a series of short notes, Madeleine discovered he was ill and wrote complaining of being unwell herself and offering her sympathy. To see him, she would walk past his lodgings and look for him at the window.

She wrote again at the beginning of March to tell him she had been in Edinburgh attending a function at the castle and was about to go off with her family for a two-week break at Bridge of Allan (north of Stirling). She advised him to go away himself and rest, but not in Scotland. The Isle of Wight was her suggestion; the further away the better. L'Angelier no doubt got the hint, but tried to see her before the family set out and he walked to Blythswood Square in the hope that she would see him and perhaps let him in the house. She did, and wrote later to tell him so, but only from her window. She had made no attempt to meet face-to-face. In her letter she advised him to wait until she returned around 20 March.

But L'Angelier was still feeling the effects of being so seriously ill. If anyone needed to escape Glasgow it was probably him. He decided to pay a visit to Edinburgh, where he stayed for around eight days, taking the opportunity whilst there to dine with Mary Perry's sister, Jane Towers, and her husband at Portobello. The dinner table conversation revolved around his recent illnesses and his belief he had succumbed only after drinking cocoa. It was a conversation they were perhaps meant to remember. By 17 March, with his health much improved, he was back in Glasgow. He did not linger long. Disappointed at discovering no letters from Madeleine waiting for him on his return, he was back on the road within two days. He told fellow Frenchman Amadee Thuau of his plan to travel over to Bridge of Allan and stay there for several days, and left instructions with his landlady to forward any letters addressed to him.

The fact that the Smith family had been staying in the same place was incidental. He knew the family's travel arrangements and was all too well aware that as he arrived they would probably be back in Glasgow. But Madeleine had promised to write on her return to Blythswood Square. For L'Angelier, the letter was extremely important. They had not met by this time for most of March, and he harboured hopes that the break away had helped rekindle the affair. Besides, he still had all her letters.

What he did not know was that on 12 March, Madeleine and William Minnoch had become formally engaged and set their wedding date for the following June. Madeleine had every intention of L'Angelier never finding out, leastways not until she had those letters back in her possession. She had no intention of resurrecting a love affair, only of finding a way to finally end it. L'Angelier had become a serious problem, one that would be solved if only he would return her letters. She had tried the hard-line approach, which had proved fruitless. Now, it seems, she resolved to try a softer approach. Obviously it involved deceit, but with the wedding day set there was little time and she could ill afford niceties. It would only be days before the news of her engagement seeped out. It appears she decided a mendacious approach would be sufficient to convince L'Angelier that he did not need to retain the letters to keep her in his life. To that end she sent him a letter arranging a meeting at Blythswood Square on Thursday night, 19 March. Unfortunately, Madeleine was not aware that he had left Glasgow. The letter was sent on, but he did not receive it until Friday morning (the 20th). Apparently unconcerned, he wrote to Mary Perry to tell her he was away from his lodgings and mentioned the missed appointment in passing: 'I should have come to see some one last night, but the letter came too late, so we are both disappointed.'

Madeleine was more concerned than he was, and wrote a second undated letter: 'Why my beloved, did you not come to me? Oh, my beloved, are you ill? I shall wait again tomorrow night – same hour and arrangement.'

This L'Angelier received on the Sunday morning (the 22nd). He immediately packed his bags and headed for the railway station. Unfortunately, the only train he could catch that morning took him to Coatbridge. From there he walked to Glasgow, arriving at Franklin Place at around 8.00 pm. He told landlady Ann Duthie the letter had brought him back, but that he intended to return to Bridge of Allan the next morning. An hour later, he left his lodgings and set off, she believed, to Blythswood Square.

But L'Angelier knew the Smith house and its routines well by this time. Religious observance was mandatory for both family and servants. Sunday meant church in the morning and prayers in the evening, always starting at nine o'clock. So, if he had intended to meet Madeleine, as he believed her letter had arranged, it could not happen until much later. He therefore made a detour and called on a friend, Mr McAllister, on Vincent Street, about a five-minute walk away from the Smith house. Unfortunately, McAllister was not at home and according to the house servant, L'Angelier left there around 9.20 pm.

He next surfaces at around half past two in the morning ringing the door-bell to his lodgings and in some distress. Ann Duthie helping him to his room, he complained of pains in his stomach and began vomiting. She made him tea but he was too ill to drink. At around 5.00 am he started with chronic diarrhoea and she went out to fetch the nearest doctor. It happened to be a Doctor James Stevens, but unfortunately he too was ill and refused to turn out. He advised her to give him hot water and drops of laudanum. This had little effect, and at 7.00 am she was back knocking at his door, and this time Doctor Stevens followed her to Franklin Place. He found L'Angelier complaining of feeling cold and in considerable pain. The doctor gave him morphia, which made him vomit again, and applied a mustard poultice to his stomach. He left at around half past eight and returned to the house at 11.15 am. But when the landlady let the doctor into the bedroom, L'Angelier was dead.

The last request he made before his death was to Ann Duthie. Perhaps realizing just how seriously ill he was, he asked that she send someone to Renfrew Street and fetch his friend, Mary Perry. In the circumstances it seems illogical. Why send for her and not the love of his life, Madeleine Smith? What was so important at such a point of crisis that the only person he wanted near him was, in effect, no more than a trusted friend? Or was it that she was an innocent being drawn by design into a very personal drama? Either way, it was all too late; she never got to talk to the dying man. But feeling morally implicated in L'Angelier's life, Mary felt obliged to carry news of the death to the Smiths. She arrived at the Blythswood Square house in the early afternoon. It was Madeleine who took her into the drawing room, but for whatever reason, Mary insisted on only talking with her mother. Madeleine was made to wait until she had left before being told of the death.

Back at 11 Franklin Place, Doctor Stevens had called for a second opinion before signing the death certificate. L'Angelier's own doctor, Hugh Thomson, was called in, and between the two of them they carried out an external examination. It was inconclusive, but neither felt satisfied that the cause was natural. Later that same day, L'Angelier's employers approached Doctor Thomson at his home, expressed their concerns over the death and requested a post-mortem be carried out. He agreed, in an unofficial capacity, to call on Doctor Stevens and have him brought back to Franklin Place so that both could carry out a full autopsy.

As part of that examination, the stomach contents were removed and a report sent to the Procurator-Fiscal for Lanark. The body was then released for burial. On 27 March, the Procurator-Fiscal in turn decided a further examination was required and the two doctors were called into his office. At that meeting, the stomach contents, sealed in a bottle, were handed over to a Doctor Penny, Professor of Chemistry at Anderson's University in Glasgow, and four days later the body was exhumed from a vault in the city's Ramshorn Church. The examination by Dr Penny discovered arsenic, and no small amount either. According to his report, he found eighty-two grains of arsenic in the stomach contents alone. Death would normally be caused by somewhere in the region of four to six grains (approx. 260-390mg). Examination of the various body organs then discovered arsenic in every one, though the quantity was never measured.

Whilst all this was ongoing, the letters written by Madeleine to L'Angelier had become a contentious point, both for the police and the Smith family. At the time of his death, it is fair to say only a select few knew of their existence: Madeleine obviously, Mary Perry through her association with L'Angelier, and the chancellor to the French consulate in Glasgow, Auguste Vauvert De Mean. He was a man Emile L'Angelier had befriended back in 1854, and had known of the clandestine affair and the love letters since the late summer of 1856. When told of the Frenchman's death, like Mary Perry, he made straight for Blythswood Square. There, only a few hours after Mary Perry's visit, he met with James Smith and acquainted him with the fact that L'Angelier had died in possession of numerous letters written to him by his daughter. He advised James Smith to retrieve these letters before they could do the family any damage. L'Angelier, he told Smith, would not have deliberately hidden them; nor had he, as far as he knew, made a secret of their existence nor of their content. Clearly, he was concerned that Madeleine and her entire family would be drawn into a damaging scandal should they ever see the light of day. Smith obviously shared his concern, but neither man knew where L'Angelier generally kept all this correspondence. After some discussion, it was decided to begin the search at his place of work. A willing Monsieur Mean then travelled to Huggins & Co. on Bothwell Street. There, he discovered he was not alone in trying to secure these letters. Mr Huggins, the owner of the merchant warehouse, had already made the request for a post-mortem to be carried out and left instructions that any letters were to stay where they were. The disappointed chancellor made his way back to Blythswood Square the following day to convey the news that it was all too late, and to try to find out from Madeleine just how serious her affair with L'Angelier had been.

Even by this early stage of the enquiry into L'Angelier's death, rumours were rife that he had been brought back to Glasgow by a letter solely to keep an appointment with its author, Madeleine Smith. Auguste De Mean wanted to know if the gossip was true. He and Madeleine met, along with her mother, Janet. It is probably fair to say it was a difficult, at times hostile meeting. Essentially, the French chancellor was acting on behalf of her father, who clearly had no knowledge of this long, secret love affair. He needed to know if he could contradict the whispered speculation on the streets and offer up an alternative version. He could not. Madeleine readily admitted her involvement in the long-standing affair, but insisted L'Angelier could not have returned to see her on the Sunday night. The source of all the rumour, she insisted, was a letter written inviting him to visit on the Saturday, an appointment he did not keep. The chancellor did not believe her, and told her so. He had a point. To travel from Bridge of Allan to Glasgow in such a hurry without there being some prior arrangement to do so seemed illogical.

The police began to see it the same way. Once they discovered the existence of these letters, they set about discovering exactly where they all were. It took a little time, but diligent work eventually found letters on his person, in his office desk, at his lodgings and inside a travel bag left at the lodging house at Bridge of Allan. In total there were around 300, all written by Madeleine, most retained inside their envelopes, the postmarks dating the correspondence from April 1855 up until his death.

On Thursday, 26 March, Madeleine Smith disappeared. Why has never been explained, but at 7.00 am that morning servants discovered she had left the house. She was found just after 2.00 pm by William Minnoch, who at this stage was not fully aware of her involvement with L'Angelier, and her brother, John, onboard a local steamer travelling toward the village of Row (Rhu) and the Smiths' country house, 'Rowaleyn'. She offered up no explanation as to why, or what she had intended to do. All three completed the journey, then returned to Glasgow that same day. She was finally arrested five days later.

Her trial began on 30 June 1857 at the High Court of Justiciary, Edinburgh, before Mr Justice Clerk and Lords Handyside and Ivory. It was a show trial from the start, with huge crowds assembled in Parliament Square on each of the eight days it took to hear evidence and reach a verdict. Madeleine, accused of attempted murder by the administration of poison on 19 or 20 February 1857, again on 22 or 23 February and then actual murder on 23 March, pleaded not guilty.

From the outset, the trial was only ever going to focus on three key issues: the love affair, poison and motive. The affair was undeniable, confirmed in detail by the letters, which were read out to the court. However, as the prosecution pointed out, L'Angelier's voice was never heard as his letters, which the court knew had been in existence at the end of February, were never found. Madeleine, they believed, had destroyed them. They may have been correct. But the defence, ably mounted by Mr George Young and Mr Moncrieff, was never really pressed on the subject. From the outset, they accepted her letters alone were conclusive evidence of a long, passionate and at times duplicitous affair, and never attempted to deny it. Only the last letter written, the one that had found its way to his lodgings at Bridge of Allan, was contentious. The prosecution used this to show L'Angelier had returned to Glasgow on the strength of its content. This, they argued, was the most important letter written by Madeleine Smith. It was the letter that had drawn him to his death on the Sunday (22 March), and that is still persuasive today. But, as was much debated in court, the letter was undated. Madeleine's insistence that it was written inviting L'Angelier to a meeting on the Saturday, not the Sunday, could not be disproved, which effectively nullified its evidential importance.

What proved by far the most difficult obstacle for her defence was the poison. It transpired during the trial that Madeleine had bought arsenic on three separate occasions in the first quarter of 1857. All were provable transactions. Since the introduction of The Sale of Arsenic Regulation Act in 1851, anyone buying the poison had to sign a register maintained by the selling shop. The arsenic itself also had to be coloured blue or black by the addition of either soot or indigo. Madeleine Smith had signed that register at Murdoch Brothers, druggists, Sauchiehall Street, on 21 February 1857 when she bought sixpence worth of arsenic (1½oz). She also returned to the shop three days later to ask why the arsenic was black. On 6 March she signed the register at Mr John Currie's druggist shop, also on Sauchiehall Street, where she bought another sixpence worth, which was coloured blue, and repeated the process at the same shop on 18 March. There could thus be no disputing that she had had the means in her possession to commit murder. To the shop owners, she had given the extermination of rats as the purpose for the purchases, which was legitimate in Victorian Britain at that time. In her written statement to the court (she did not take the stand), she stated its use was actually for cosmetic purposes; a not unheard of practice by ladies at that time, and not uncommon. Its supposedly restorative qualities when used in water to wash the face were well-advertised.

L'Angelier had been verified as being ill by his landlady in early February (no specific date was given), again on 23 February and finally on 22/23 March. The first incident obviously could not be shown to have been caused by arsenic poisoning, but the other two episodes certainly could. Clearly, the purchases placed her in an insidious position, though it was only the March illness that offered any tangible proof. This was bourne out by Doctor Penny, the man who analyzed the stomach contents after the post-mortem. When he took the stand, her innocence looked extremely questionable.

According to his evidence, although some eighty-two grains of arsenic had been found in his stomach, the amount of liquid vomited meant the amount actually swallowed would have been substantially more; maybe as much as 200 grains (around ½oz). But to take in such a quantity it would have needed to be suspended in a liquid: water, tea or coffee possibly, but he said these were unlikely. Arsenic is not soluble and would have needed to be placed in suspension to avoid being detected. Cocoa, if boiled in the liquid, would have sufficed. Doctor Penny added that it was unlikely to have been arsenic coated by soot, as that would leave behind a blackened deposit. However, indigo-dyed arsenic, certainly the type used by Mr Currie's druggist, would not do so.

It was known that Madeleine took cocoa, and that L'Angelier on his visits could well have shared it. So she had the means; did she have the motive? There has always been an argument that she needed L'Angelier alive; after all, he had her letters. If he was not alive, how would they have been retrieved? Essentially, this was the gist of the defence argument to the jury. The Frenchman had effectively blackmailed her into maintaining their relationship. He had behaved badly toward her and had taken advantage of her in the earlier stages of the love affair. The letters, those damning written documents, would expose her to ridicule and scandal if ever discovered and published. Therefore, her defence said, she had to keep him alive and play a devious, deceitful game to obtain them. Guile was her weapon, not murder, as that would not suit her purpose.

The jury agreed, and after one of the longest trials in Scottish history at that time they gave her the benefit of the doubt. After a half-hour consultation, they returned a not proven verdict and Madeleine Smith walked free from the court.

But did she do it? That is a question much debated over the years, with various arguments for and against. From my own point of view, I find it incredible that a man would make the dash back from Bridge of Allan to Glasgow, being forced to walk part of the way from Coatbridge, then not go to see the love of his life. There can be no other reason for making the journey, to my mind, unless he felt certain that he would be meeting Madeleine Smith that Sunday night. I therefore believe her claim that the letter she wrote had been sent with the intention of arranging that meet for Saturday night was a lie. The puzzle is just exactly where L'Angelier was after half past nine that night? He knew the household and their rituals so well. No meeting was likely until Madeleine's sister was asleep, which meant any meeting had to have been very late. Arsenic takes effect up to an hour after consumption. He arrives back at his lodgings between 2.00–2.30 am. Whether she poisoned him or not, the time means he could not have taken the arsenic before 1.00 am. Ann Duthie, who had seen the previous vomiting attacks, describes the liquid he threw up as being 'as before'. In other words, greenish and thick, like gruel. That suggests to me he had possibly taken cocoa, which puts him in the Smith house. Many accounts of this murder have suggested they met outside her bedroom window and she passed the drink out to him. I cannot believe that. She was extremely careful about being seen in his company, she had warned him about tapping on her window when sister Janet was sleeping in her room and the road outside was a public space. Besides, reading through her letters she clearly states that she can get him into the house. I believe that is exactly what she did. Bringing him in through the front door allowed her to take him into the drawing room, where they were away from the rest of the household. This also meant all their meetings were held late at night, if not the early hours, otherwise detection by the household would have been too easy. Like the Lord Advocate who prosecuted the case said, that gave her the opportunity, and buying arsenic three times made her culpable.

Would L'Angelier's death have prevented her obtaining her letters? No. The Smiths were wealthy and the class system worked in their favour, otherwise the chancellor to the French Consulate would not have beaten a path to their door when he knew of L'Angelier's demise. If there had been no suspicion about the death, it is likely he would have succeeded in his endeavours to retrieve the letters and return them to Madeleine's father. Murder, for her at that moment in time, was a perfect solution. She had become engaged to William Minnoch, set the wedding for June and had known when she agreed to the marriage that if L'Angelier refused to walk away it could never happen. So, she certainly had motive.

If not her, then him? Did he commit suicide? To me the evidence does not support it, but cannot be entirely dismissed. He certainly had a knowledge of arsenic. He had perhaps even used it, and there are strange illnesses in his past that appear to have shown similar symptoms. But the quantity taken was extremely large and could not have been swallowed in its dry state very easily. There is, however, an argument that he never did meet Madeleine that night but returned to his lodgings, perhaps around midnight (he had a key to get in), drank the poison, then left and returned when it had taken effect, not using his key the second time to create the illusion of having been murdered. Certainly, he had discussed poison, or the possibility of himself being poisoned, with Mary Perry, the Towers at Portobello and some of his work colleagues, according to evidence presented in court. So the suggestion that it was suicide is not necessarily beyond the bounds of possibility.

Weighing up all the evidence, I feel, like the jury, that the case against Madeleine Smith is impossible to prove.

*Chapter 2*

# Bradford's Jack the Ripper

## *The murder of John Gill, 1888*

William Barrett had been born in Cononley around 1866. Set in the Aire valley south of Skipton, the village had proven a safe, secure place to live during the second half of the nineteenth century. A church-going family, the Barretts had educated their son at the nearby Primitive Methodist School. In return, he readily embraced the church and its teachings, choosing to become a Sunday school teacher in his late teens. By his early twenties, he had married into the Metcalfe printing family and was working for local landowners and farmers the Wolfendens. For Barrett, working in the local textile mill was never an option. The Wolfendens had offered him a home before he married, and working for them at the Ashfield Dairy on Manningham Lane, Bradford, was an easy decision. Through his work with the church, he had an easy way with people and enjoyed working outdoors. So the job of milkman in Manningham on the outskirts of Bradford suited him well. He enjoyed the work, made friends easily and quickly settled into his new life. It would prove life-changing in more ways than one.

The milkman's role at that time, unlike today, did not involve door-to-door bottle delivery. The work was arduous, and every working day was a long slog. For William Barrett, it started at 6.30 am when he arrived at the stables off Manningham Lane to feed and groom the dray horse. He went home again for breakfast and then back to the stable to collect the horse and walk it over to the dairy. Once there, he would harness it to the milk cart before taking it down to the railway station to meet the morning milk train. After helping to unload it, the milk, all in pails, would be divided between the needs of the dairy and those of his customers on the early morning round. The cart would then be loaded and his first house-to-house round would begin. At around 9.00 am, he would be back at the dairy to reload and start his second delivery round, which would normally take until about eleven o'clock. The cart would then be unharnessed back at the dairy and the horse returned to the stables, and he would begin work with the cream extractor. At around 5.00 pm the process would be repeated (but with no house deliveries), and he would be back at the railway station to meet the 5.40 pm train which brought in more milk for the dairy's evening work. His day ended at around 8.00 pm, and he arrived back at home some half an hour later.

Thursday, 27 December 1888 began the same way as any other for William Barrett, and, other than the dairy needing him to work later to help in the making of butter, he expected it to follow a similar routine. Christmas had passed, demand had slackened off and the daily round involved less work. It was also colder and the local school was closed for the holidays. Barrett knew when he started the day that he would probably have company on his early round. Eight-year-old schoolboy John Gill liked travelling on the milk cart, and when he saw it pass his house on Thorncliffe Road at half past seven that morning, en route to the station, he ran out to clamber on board. It was not the first time either; riding the cart was a special treat and Barrett liked the company. The two had developed a routine. If it was a school day he would send the boy home in plenty of time for breakfast. If a holiday, then he would normally let him stay longer and give him something to eat back at the dairy. But on this particular day it was frosty, the roads were icy, the horse was less sure-footed and the boy wanted to be off, making a slide in the icy conditions. So Barrett dropped him off around half past eight at Walmer Villas, a reasonably wealthy area off Manningham Lane and not far from the boy's home. It was the last time John Gill would be seen alive.

His frantic parents, after searching long into the night, placed an advertisement in the following day's edition of the *Bradford Daily Telegraph*:

'Lost, on Thursday morning, boy John Gill, aged 8. Was last seen sliding in Walmer Villas at 8.30 am. Has on navy blue top coat (with brass buttons on) midshipmans cap, plaid knicker-bocker suit, laced boots, red and black stockings; complexion fair. Home 41 Thorncliffe Road.'

Throughout Friday, 28 December the search continued. News of the missing schoolboy had by this time reached the wider community, and by early afternoon, large crowds had gathered outside the Gill household. Police, in ever-increasing numbers, were brought in to help maintain order and control the throng. But nothing was found by nightfall, and for the Gill family it meant a second night without sleep.

At half past six the following morning, William Barrett arrived at the Gill house to ask for an update and offer help if needed. But by this time most search avenues had been exhausted. Unless the police came up with something new, continuing the search probably seemed futile. Manningham at this time was a thriving, cosmopolitan suburb outside Bradford, with a mix of housing, back-to-backs alongside Victorian villas. It was a place where rich and poor co-existed comfortably, and its main thoroughfare, Manningham Lane, was a booming place of business. It was thus a wide and varied area to try to search for a missing schoolboy. For the family it was an impossible task. Unfortunately for them, within the hour the search would be over.

A short distance from the back of the Gills' house was Mellor Road, from where a short, narrow 10ft-wide entry ran into what was known locally as Back Mellor Street. At the end of this stood a small complex of buildings centred around a coach house (a garage-like building), fronted by two large wooden doors and flanked on either side by stables. The stable on the right was owned by butcher James Berwick, and opposite was a manure pit. At around 7.00 am that Saturday morning (29 December), Joseph Bucke, whose job it was to turn out the horse and clean out the stable for the butcher each morning, noticed a strange bundle propped against the door to the coach house. First impressions suggested old discarded clothes, but closer inspection revealed the mutilated corpse of a child.

The first policeman on the scene, PC Haigh, made a cursory examination of the bundle where it lay. It was enough to confirm that the body, wrapped in an overcoat, was that of a young boy. The corpse was naked and the legs had been cut off and laid beneath the torso, which lay on its back. A pair of braces had been used to hold the bundle together, and the stomach had been ripped open from the abdomen up to the throat. Deciding it was way beyond his pay grade, PC Haigh left the bundle in situ and immediately sent for Doctor Major, the local GP, whose surgery was close by. Understandably less squeamish, he made a more detailed examination and in the process discovered the boy's ears where missing and that his boots had been pushed inside the stomach cavity. Haigh, on realizing the gravity of the discovery, then tried to have the scene protected from sightseers and organised for police surgeon Samuel Lodge to be brought to the scene.

Well aware of being in a crime scene, Lodge's examination was of necessity brief. But essentially he concurred with the GP, and after a lengthy consultation with the missing boy's parents, who by this time had been made aware of a body having been found, confirmed it was that of John Gill.

That in turn launched a murder enquiry. The boy's parents, as was routine, were the first to be interviewed. William Barrett was next, and as possibly the last person to have seen the boy before his disappearance he was, no doubt, an obvious suspect. That need not have been a problem; he and the boy were often on the early morning round together. But surprisingly, by ten minutes past nine that same morning the young milkman had become the only suspect. Obviously not satisfied with how he had explained away the boy's failure to complete the round that morning, police had taken him into custody. From the outset, there seems to have been little doubt in their minds that Barrett had been less than truthful, though quite how they could have reacted so quickly with so little available evidence seems a little questionable. Nevertheless, they detained him in custody and let it be known before the day was out that they were confident they had also found the murder site.

This lay some 150 yards from Ashfield Dairy and was the stable housing the horse used by William Barrett every morning of his working week. Situated in an area known as Belle Vue, behind rows of back-to-back housing and a local landmark, the Servants Hall, it was detached, built to house two horses, incorporated a small coach house and had a wide hayloft above the stabling. It was hardly surprising that Barrett had fallen under suspicion once this place was known to the police. Fronted by a wall, with no gas lighting within, a sink between the two stalls and a gutter running its length to take water, it was an obvious and reasonable assumption to have made. But finding the proof that would support it as the place where John Gill died was not going to be that easy.

Though from the outset, it appears James Withers, Chief Constable of Bradford, thought otherwise. He deployed policemen to the site within hours of the body's discovery and carried out a thorough inspection that went on throughout the day. The results proved disappointing. There were no clear bloodstains, but there was a suspiciously wet floor. There was also a large piece of canvas with brown staining, that could or could not have been used during the dissection, and a small hammer. The canvas sheeting and the hammer were sent off for scientific examination. The floor, he could only speculate about. But, perhaps more importantly, what struck Withers particularly was just how dark it was in there. With no gas lighting, he had been forced to stumble around using matches to light his way. He quickly realized that meant the place would have needed to be well lit to carry out the kind of dissection he had seen. In turn, the use of light late at night may well have attracted the curious and the light sleepers. House-to-house enquiries were organized for the following day.

These enquiries revealed a few individuals with vague recollections of seeing lights around the stables but none with perfect recall. Pinning down any sort of precise time for these lights, at this stage of the enquiry, proved more than difficult, but Withers was prepared to be patient. House calls, he knew, were time-consuming, particularly in an area known for housing shift workers. But perseverance usually paid rewards. There was also another avenue he wanted explored. The wet flooring had clearly troubled him. It seemed to him that the stable floor had been washed or swilled at the wrong time of the day. He instructed officers to pull up the flagstones. If it was the murder site, it had most likely been washed to remove blood. The logic was obviously well-founded, but the results were disappointing: nothing visible was found. Soil samples were taken, quickly sifted and analyzed. What they revealed was equally disappointing. No blood – animal or human – had been spilt in that stable at any point in the recent past. Determining the site to be the place where the boy had met his death was proving problematic.

However, there was an argument in favour of it being the site where the body lay after the dissection had been carried out. Police Constable Arthur Kirk had been the beat bobby on duty throughout the night of 28 December into the early hours of the 29th. He was responsible for walking the beat where the butcher's stable stood and he had checked the stable door where the body had been found on five separate occasions, from the start of his shift at 9.00 pm until his final check at 4.30 am, and found it locked each time. The bundle had not been there on any of those occasions, which meant the killer could only have placed the body between 4.30 am and its discovery at 7.00 am. If nearby Belle Vue stables, where the Chief Constable had been searching, had only been the storage point, then the killer had a two-and-a-half-hour window of opportunity to carry the body from Belle Vue to Berwick's stable.

The surrounding streets housed the textile mill shift workers. For many that meant rising around 5.00 am and walking to work between six and seven o'clock, so anyone carrying a bundle to Berwick's stable around those times was at great risk of being observed. The Chief Constable questioned whether or not the killer could have done so without being seen, but probably accepted that it had to be a possibility. The investigation was nevertheless widened to try to find those on the streets between these key times.

Whilst that continued, Samuel Lodge carried out a full post-mortem on the boy's body. What he found was disturbing. In his report to police, he stated that, in his opinion, the boy had died as a result of two stab wounds to the left chest; both had penetrated muscle and bone and would have resulted in death. All the mutilations took place later, probably using a different knife. The stab wounds themselves had been made using a weapon that was broad-bladed and not too sharp, but had severed the aorta, whilst the dissection itself could only have been carried out using a much stronger, sharper-bladed knife and something like a hammer or mallet to separate the joints and remove the limbs. The boy's ears had been removed, as had both legs, severed through the thigh. His penis, parts of the intestine, heart, lungs and liver had also been removed; the latter had been dried out before being placed back inside the body cavity, along with some of the other organs. The body, in its entirety, along with these removed organs, had also been washed externally and internally and all the body's blood carefully drained away. Lodge estimated some 5lb (2.5kg) of blood had been removed from a body weighing only 50lb (25kg): 'The body was blanched, all the blood having been drained away.'

Strangely, he also found the throat had not been cut, nor were blood stains found on the clothing, with the exception of the boy's shirt collar. The blood found there was substantial and still damp when examined. Death, he believed, had been some twenty-four hours earlier than when he first saw the body. He added that after inspecting the clothing found with the body inside the bundle, he had found no tears in the fabric: 'Neither jacket, waistcoat, or shirt bear any cuts and it is therefore evident that they had been removed before the stabs were inflicted. The trousers indicate that they had not been removed until after the fatal blow.'

Also found amongst the body parts, and used in part to help keep them all together, was a piece of canvas or sacking with the words 'W.MASON, DERBY ROAD, LIVERPOOL' stencilled across it. Chief Constable Withers sent two detectives over to the city to try to ascertain just where it had originated (but that was never confirmed).

Meanwhile, with Barrett still in custody, police descended on his home in a search for the murder weapon. They found and removed a bread knife, took away his clothes, then went on to the dairy, where they found an old hatchet, enough evidence, they decided, to hold him on suspicion of murder. At 4.00 pm on that Saturday (29 December) he made his first appearance in the magistrates' court. It was a short hearing, the court remanding him back into custody whilst enquiries continued. The inquest into the death then formerly opened on Monday, 31 December and adjourned until 25 January 1889.

Before any of that could happen, Barrett was back in the dock at Bradford's Police Court on 2 January. Press coverage of the proceedings gave local people their first opportunity to read more detail about the murder and the evidence against Barrett, a man most had refused to believe guilty of any involvement in the boy's death. Chief Constable Withers, who obviously did not share their conviction, acted for the police, solicitor John Craven represented William Barrett and a Mr Armitage presided over the proceedings. After outlining the circumstances of the case, Barrett's occupation and involvement with the murdered boy and the various subsequent searches – all of which was pretty much general knowledge by this time – some time was spent hearing how the body had been found and subsequently examined by the police surgeon. By far the most interesting witnesses who spoke were those light sleepers and early risers the Chief Constable had sent his officers out to find. There were not many, and their evidence certainly was vague, but they did give credence to his belief that the body could have been dismembered in Barrett's stable, despite the lack of blood evidence.

The matron of the Servants Hall, the building overlooking the dairy's stable, told the court that whilst she had seen nothing untoward, she had heard movement. According to her testimony, the bedroom she slept in overlooked the buildings below, and sounds travelled well. Between 1.00 am and 3.00 am on Saturday, 29 December she claimed to have heard the distinctive sounds, in eight to ten-minute bursts, of someone sweeping the stable floor. That same individual eventually walked off in the direction of Manningham Lane.

Lizzie Jefferson, a servant in the same building, told of the stable having a window that looked out onto the scullery, where every morning she began work. On the Friday, 28 December, she claimed the stable was lit from inside at around 6.00 am.

Local photographer Henry Ledgard, a man familiar with the stable on Belle Vue because he passed it almost every night, was used to always finding it closed up and in total darkness. But on the Thursday night of the boy's disappearance, he saw the stable door open at around 10.30 pm, a clear, low light and a man he could not identify stooping down just inside.

There were others, their testimonies when taken collectively suggestive of the fact that over the night of Thursday and Friday, 27 and 28 December, something unusual could have been happening in Barrett's stable. But it did not place him there. In fact, after Borough analyst Mr Rimmington took the stand to explain his results for all the items that had been found and examined, there seemed to be no case at all. Nothing, he told the court, had been found to show the presence of any blood, nor had close inspection of the sink and drains in the stable, along with soil deposits from beneath the flagstone floor, revealed a definite murder site. Only the boy's stomach contents, according to Rimmington's testimony, offered up a clue: they contained undigested fruit cake. Today, we know that means death occurred within two hours or so of the boy eating it. Back in 1889, forensics was still in its infancy. The court therefore adjourned without reaching any definite conclusion.

Two days later, John Gill's funeral took place at Windhill Cemetery, and on 9 January, William Barrett was formerly charged with his murder and was back in the dock. The only new evidence came from three witnesses. A butcher, Richard Manuel, testified that he had seen Barrett standing at the door of the Belle Vue stable on the Friday night of 28 December at around 11.45 pm. He described the clothing he wore as cord trousers, a sleeved waistcoat and a cap, all of which had been recovered by police and found to have been freshly washed: suspicious certainly, but far from damning. Wilson Riley, a dairyman who worked alongside Barrett, told the court he had seen him on several occasions throughout the day of the boy's disappearance and had visited the stable himself during that time, and saw nothing strange or suspicious. He added that the stable was unlocked and open because the key had been lost. William, the sole key-holder, had lost the key some days earlier, which meant access to the stable would have been easy for anyone who knew the area. But Police Constable Kirk, the policeman who had checked the Berwick stable as part of his beat throughout the early hours of Saturday, 29 December, had, it transpired, also checked the outbuildings at Belle Vue. He told the court that he had checked Barrett's stable every hour between 10.00 pm and 5.30 am on the night of 27 and 28 December. At no time was anyone there, and the stable, he told the magistrates, was definitely locked.

It was a long day, and after listening to a further sixty-four witnesses, magistrates adjourned for twenty-four hours. It seems that other than the three witnesses mentioned above, nothing particularly new was brought to the court. At 3.00 pm the following day, dissatisfied with the weight of evidence police had produced, the magistrates declared there was no *prima facie* case to answer. William Barrett was released back into the community.

The matter did not end there, however. The court may have decided that the evidence presented by police was merely circumstantial, which it was, but the inquest had not. There had been a deliberate decision made by the coroner to allow time for the magistrates' court to continue after the inquest's initial adjournment, possibly to await that court's verdict.

Once concluded, and within days of Barrett's release from custody, the inquest was reopened. A further three adjournments followed, during which time it heard testimony from the same witnesses, with one single exception: John Thomas Dyer.

Employed to clean shoes by a Major Churchill at his home at Walmer Villas, he told the coroner that on the morning of the body's discovery he had seen a man carrying a bundle over both arms at around 6.05 am. That man, he asserted, had been William Barrett. According to Dyer, he knew Barrett from his milk round and had spoken to him that morning but had been ignored. Barrett, he told the court, had emerged from a gate at the Orphans home, Belle Vue, and walked in front of him toward Manningham Lane holding some sort of parcel in his arms. He crossed over near the Belle Vue Hotel and walked down an entry that would have taken him toward the place where John Gill's body was found.

This was a damning piece of evidence, if true, and supported the Chief Constable's earlier assertion that if the killer moved John Gill's body in the early hours of 29 December he could well have been seen. Unfortunately for the police, Dyer was a man of low intellect, prone to telling tall stories and not easily believed. He had also not told his story to anyone for several days. Fanny Turrel, the major's cook, was the first person he told. He had then kept silent until after the Magistrates' Court had released Barrett from Armley Jail before informing local police. The cook confirmed she had known but probably doubted the veracity of his story and had never discussed it with anyone else. However, it helped sway the inquest jury and they, unlike the magistrates, felt there was a case to answer and returned a verdict of murder against Barrett, who was rearrested.

The trial was set for the West Riding Assize Court, Leeds, on 12 March 1889, but never actually took place; leastways, not in a conventional sense. Instead, the case became a matter for legal argument in a closed courtroom between prosecution counsel Mr Forbes QC and defence counsel Mr Waddy QC. They both appeared before Mr Commissioner White QC, whose job it was to hear legal argument as to whether or not the case should proceed. In essence, the defence were arguing that as the Magistrates' Court had thrown out the case, then a verdict of not guilty should stand against the coroner's verdict. The prosecution offered the court three options:

1. Apply to the Attorney General for leave to enter *nolle prosequi* (be unwilling to pursue) upon the coroner's inquisition.

2. Leave the coroner's inquisition in place without calling upon Barrett to enter a plea.
3. Call upon Barrett to enter a plea and if that were done the prosecution would offer no evidence.

The court chose the third option, and Barrett was brought into the dock and told to enter a plea. He pleaded not guilty. A jury was then sworn in, and Mr Forbes stood before them and said he would offer no evidence. The jury were then instructed to return a not guilty verdict, which they did, and Barrett was released from custody. He left the courthouse by a back entrance to avoid the huge crowds that had gathered in the streets outside.

For him, the case was over but financially the cost had been high, and was quoted in local newspapers as being around £500 (£44,900 today). So, along with his employer John Wolfenden, Reverend J.P. Ashborne of Skipton, his mother, Mr Haswell of Kildwick and a large party of well-wishers, he began a roadshow. The party travelled around Skipton, Keighley and Bradford's villages, addressing large crowds and explaining the case and its outcome. Donations were collected at each destination, the money raised put toward payment to his legal team.

As Barrett continued his fund-raising efforts, speculation, which to be fair had been ongoing for some weeks, was rife as to exactly who could have murdered John Gill. For many it was a 'Jack the Ripper' killing. The Whitechapel murders had been headline news in the north of England, just as in the south. Lurid details of his murders and his victims were widely publicized, so for many the manner of the boy's death fitted with the depravity exhibited by the London killer. Even Bradford's police entertained the idea that Jack could have travelled north, calling in experts from London to examine the body whilst Barrett was in custody. They, obviously, threw the notion out. But Jack the Ripper, as far as the local press were concerned, had actually been in Manningham around the time of the killing. They cited the strange case of the Cahills on Heaton Road.

On 26 December, the Cahill couple went out to the annual servants' ball held at the Alexandra Hotel. As the dancing that night did not begin until 11.00 pm, they had stayed overnight, not returning to their home until the following day, 27 December (the morning of Gill's disappearance) at around 10.00 am. Upon entering the house, they found an open umbrella on the floor in the hall, a dress belonging to Mrs Cahill hanging from the ceiling of the lounge, other pieces of her clothing carefully arranged on a high-backed chair topped by a bonnet, and spread across a table a variety of household items and a pencil-written note, which read: 'Half past nine. Look out Jack the Ripper has been here.'

On the card's reverse was: 'I have removed down to the canal side. Please drop in. Yours Truly SUICIDE.'

On the same table was a large tin containing water, some of which had been deliberately spilt across the table top. The living room furniture had all been moved around the room, the contents of a large cupboard emptied out onto the floor and a number of boxes of matches placed on their ends around crossed knives.

The couple called in the police, who perhaps understandably were a little reticent, choosing to keep these details to themselves once news of the murder became public knowledge, especially with the Cahills' house only half a mile away from where the body had been discovered. Though they must have known that word would spread without their help, as it did, over the following weeks. The matter was dismissed as having no relevance by the Chief Constable, who was perhaps right, it certainly not being done by Jack the Ripper, whose *modus operandi* never involved burglary. But the disarray at the Cahills' house could have had a relevance to his murder scenes.

It strikes me as odd that such an event would take place just before the discovery of the body of John Gill. It was almost as if someone wanted to create the impression that his murder was the work of a profligate, skilled killer. A man invisible to the law. However, I would doubt very much that the Whitechapel killer caught a train north himself. More likely it was the work of a devious local mind.

But was William Barrett innocent? It is obviously impossible to say at this distance from events, but there are a few questions that were never answered at the time. John Wolfenden, Barrett's employer, told the local press after the court hearing that the wrapping around John Gill's body with the words 'W. MASON, DERBY ROAD, LIVERPOOL' was used to carry feed to the dairy's horse. By default, that means it had to have been in the Belle Vue stable. He also stated that the stable had one key and Barrett was the key holder, an important fact to know after dairyman Wilson Riley's evidence suggested the key had been lost and the stable left open. Yet according to the beat bobby, PC Kirk, he checked the stable door throughout the night of 27/28 December and it was always locked. If that were true, and I have no reason to disbelieve him, then Barrett, who was always at the stable in the morning to sort out the horse, must have always had a key. In other words, it could never have been lost.

Then of course there is the evidence of all those who claimed to have seen lights in the stable in the early hours of the morning, or had heard movement in the Belle Vue stable. There is also John Dyer: unreliable maybe, but a doubtful liar; a man who saw someone on the morning of the body's discovery carrying something overly large, and actually spoke to him. The question is, was that man William Barrett? The coroner's court seemed inclined to believe him. Certainly, if the body was dissected in the stables used by Ashfield Dairy, they were used by a man who knew the policeman's routines and timings, who swilled the floor thoroughly after doing the work and who knew just where he needed to leave the body if he wanted it to be found. This is definitely a killer determined that his work, just like that of Jack the Ripper, would be discovered.

So, was William Barrett the killer? Did he really send the boy home for breakfast, or had he forgotten it was a school holiday? And who fed him cake just before killing him?

*Chapter 3*

# The Country House Shooting

*The murder of Windsor Dudley Cecil Hambrough, 1893*

Ardlamont House stands on the tip of the Cowal peninsula on the west coast of Scotland. With Kintyre to the west, Bute to the east and the Isle of Arran just south of Ardlamont Point, it is the picturesque location it was always intended to be. Built in 1820 by Major General Lamont, Chief of clan Lamont, it is surrounded by hundreds of acres of woodland. It was no doubt intended to house the family in perpetuity. Unfortunately, the expectations of its builder had foundered somewhat on the financial failures of a later generation. By the start of 1893, the house and its estates were for sale. Looking to buy, though without any personal wealth to back the aspiration, was 33-year-old Alfred Monson, tutor and friend of Cecil Hambrough, son and heir to the Isle of Wight banking family fortune. Monson had entered into negotiations with the selling agents after renting the house, along with the shooting rights, for himself, wife Agnes, his three children and of course Cecil Hambrough. There was probably never any serious intent to buy. He needed the Hambroughs to agree, which they were never likely to do, being financially stretched themselves at this time. More likely he was looking for his young charge to be able to raise finance on the back of any future inheritance. It seems Alfred Monson was adept at manipulating others to create a financial advantage for himself.

Alfred was born to a religious and comfortably off family. Thomas Monson, his father, was the Rector of Kirby Underdale in the East Riding of Yorkshire, and his mother the daughter of Viscount Galway, which had ensured a reasonably affluent childhood. A graduate of Oxford, though some doubt has been expressed over the veracity of this claim, Alfred forged himself a life surrounded by the trappings of wealth. Exactly from where that wealth was derived has been the source of some contention over the years. Certainly, at the time he moved into Ardlamont, he was being paid a retainer of sorts by Dudley Hambrough for tutoring his son, and had been for some time, though that was about to come to an end. Unhappy with the way he believed Monson was acting with regards to his son and to himself, Dudley Hambrough made unsuccessful attempts to try to force his son to leave Monson and move back to the family home in London. Relations were strained further after Monson allowed Cecil to become a lieutenant in the West Yorkshire Regiment and not the Hants Militia, a transgression Dudley Hambrough found impossible to forgive, but it would appear was never of concern to Monson.

By 1893, 20-year-old Cecil Hambrough was essentially a part of the Monson family. He had by this time been living with them for some time, and perhaps even considered them to *be* family. Without doubt, he expressed no wish to return to the Hambrough home, which was no longer on the Isle of Wight by this time. Financial difficulties had forced the family away from Steephill Castle and onto the mainland. Living in Scotland, in a house of the stature which Ardlamont possessed, must have seemed by far the better option. The outdoor life was, for Cecil at least, to be embraced and enjoyed. The house on the Cowal peninsula, with its own beach, vast acreage and easy access to game, must have seemed heaven-sent. London could offer nothing by comparison. The situation suited him well; perhaps it suited Monson even more.

On Tuesday, 8 August 1893, Monson embarked upon a second piece of subterfuge when he met with the Paisley engineering firm of Hannah, Donald & Wilson to begin negotiations to purchase a steam yacht, the *Alert*, supposedly on behalf of Cecil. Exactly why he did this has never been fully explained, though Cecil was certainly aware of the intended acquisition. The cost of the vessel, around £1,200, was never likely to have been met. Financing through a third party was the only way the capital could be raised. Even so, Monson continued the deception when that same evening a man named Edward Scott (discovered later to be an alias), posing as an engineer, arrived at Ardlamont House, ostensibly brought to Scotland from England to inspect the vessel at a later date. Whether Cecil was aware of these doubtful credentials is unlikely, but, nevertheless, the three men seemed to get along reasonably well. The following evening, Scott dined with all the family after spending much of the day entertaining Monson's children. During that meal, and perhaps buoyed up by alcohol, one of the three suggested a little late-night fishing. Cecil Hambrough had expressed an interest in splash fishing before, and at this time of year the salmon were thought to be increasing in numbers. The greater the numbers, the greater the chance of catching them, or so the theory ran. None of the three men were in any way expert, but as splash fishing involved the use of a net, not a rod, it was probably deemed the easier way to fish effectively.

In essence, the idea is to a drop a net into the water from the back of a rowing boat. The boat is then rowed to form a wide arc, with the other end of the net secured further along the shoreline. The fish are trapped within the arc of the net. The rowing boat then sits in the centre and the oarsmen splash the water around, panicking the fish, which are in turn trapped by the net. It was usually relatively straightforward, but not so that night.

Scott, possibly because he was less of a fisherman, stayed on shore whilst Hambrough and Monson did all the rowing. They had hired a boat from Tighnabruaich's boat hirer, Daniel McKellar, which ought to have been of sufficient size for their needs, but after rowing out some distance they struck a rock and the boat capsized. After floundering in the water for several minutes, Hambrough, a non-swimmer, managed to clamber on to the rock whilst Monson swam back to shore. Once there, he met with the waiting Scott. The two men then ran back to where they knew Ardlamont's carpenter kept his own boat, retrieved it, and Monson rowed out again to find Hambrough. After some difficulties, he pulled him from the water, bundled him back into the boat and struck out for the shore. The second boat then also sank in shallower water, and after some struggle the two waded back to where Scott stood watching. They found their way back to the house around 2.00 am, where butler James Wright was waiting up for them. After Monson and Hambrough changed their clothes, they sent Wright to his bed whilst they stayed up with Scott. Monson's wife was set to catch the early morning boat to Glasgow. Time was passing, and it seemed reasonable to the three of them to sit up until she had left. A morning's shooting was suggested and agreed. So, when she left the house that morning at around 7.00 am, they followed.

Scott had no weapon, knew nothing about guns and had no intention of shooting at anything. He was to be a spectator, perhaps retrieve whatever was shot and carry it back. Monson and Hambrough were, to his mind, the experts, although Hambrough perhaps the less experienced of the two. This was borne out by his intended use of his own 20-bore shotgun, which as the party set out Monson had gone to fetch from the nearby gamekeeper's cottage, leaving Hambrough with his own 12-bore as a replacement until he could catch them up.

Just before 9.00 am, the three were all back together again and shooting commenced just south of the house. The weather by this time had deteriorated, with heavy cloud, thunder, lightning and occasional rain, making the terrain wet and more difficult to navigate. But they persevered and, according to later testimony from Auchterarder watch-maker James Dunn, who was staying at the nearby school house, they moved round from the south and crossed over a road. Scott, Dunn believed, was carrying a rabbit as they then entered a wood to the east of Ardlamont House. Hambrough broke away and walked off alone to the right-hand side of the wood, whilst Monson and Scott kept to the left. Some minutes after the three had passed from Dunn's sight, there was a single shot.

Monson and Scott were back at the house within minutes of that shot being fired. Wright, the butler, found the two of them outside the dining room. They told him Cecil Hambrough had accidentally shot himself and was dead. After some discussion, it was decided that Monson, gardener Archibald Whyte, coachman Hugh Carmichael and the butler would go to find the young lieutenant and bring his body back to the house. They took a rug to wrap him in and aid in the carrying.

The body lay on top of a turf wall, placed there, Monson told the group, by himself and Scott after they found it in the ditch which ran alongside. The presumption was he had fallen from the wall when the gun went off. At that point no-one questioned Monson's account, and the body was carried back to the house and taken up to his bedroom, where it was re-dressed and placed in bed. The local GP, Doctor MacMillan, was called, and he examined the body much later that same morning. No expert in gunshot wounds, his examination was probably cursory, though he noted that there was an absence of blackening or singeing around the wound area, suggesting the shot that killed him had not been fired close to the head. This did not, however, raise any suspicion in his mind. He was satisfied that the lieutenant had met his death as the result of a tragic accident.

Cecil Hambrough's parents were notified, not of the death but of there having been an accident. It was not until they arrived in Glasgow, twenty-four hours later, that they discovered the truth. They were met at Greenock on the Saturday morning (12 August) by Monson and his wife, Agnes, and taken to Ardlamont to view their son's body. Despite their disapproval of Monson in his tutoring of their son, it appears there was no animosity toward him in light of the death. They agreed with the eventual report perepared by Doctor MacMillan and forwarded on to the Procurator Fiscal, and arranged the funeral for the following week. Monson and John Steven, Ardlamont's estate manager, accompanied the coffin back to the Isle of Wight and Cecil Hambrough was buried at St Catherine's Church, Ventnor, on 17 August. There, the matter would have ended, and the tragic story of

Windsor Dudley Cecil Hambrough allowed to fade into obscurity, were it not for an insurance policy.

Four years earlier, Alfred Monson had been introduced to the Hambrough family as the ideal personal tutor for their son by Beresford Loftus Tottenham – 'Tot' to his friends. 'Tot' was a financial agent based in London with the seemingly impeccable background of an ex-officer in the 10th Hussars, a man who had fought for both the Turkish and Greek armies. He knew the people that mattered, moved in wealthy circles and, for Monson, would prove a vital ally in his attempt to fund a rich lifestyle. In essence, he was a moneylender with an eye for the main chance. For him, at that time, tying Monson to the Hambroughs was probably an ideal money-making opportunity. Cecil Hambrough was set to inherit once he reached the age of majority, which at that time was 21. In the intervening years, that single fact (a future inheritance) could be used as leverage to raise money. Monson was a willing enough partner. Financing a lifestyle he could ill afford created a constant need for cash. The young Hambrough, only too happy to move out of his family home and into the Monsons', seemingly raised no objections.

So in February 1893, with Cecil Hambrough only a year away from this financial windfall, Monson sued him for £800 for board, lodgings and education as the allowance from his father had ceased. The case was uncontested and Cecil, as far as is known, was a willing participant. Tottenham purchased Monson's interest in the judgement for £200, instantly releasing money into the Monson household. 'Tot' then arranged with Monson to pay the young Hambrough a £5 a week allowance, which increased to £10 when they moved to Ardlamont. Buying the Scottish estate was then raised by Monson; 'Tot' readily agreed, travelled to Scotland in July that year and set in motion the purchase. The idea was that Ardlamont would be purchased in Agnes Monson's name, in trust for Cecil. Whilst there, it appears Tottenham also agreed to loan Hambrough up to £1,000, if required, on the proviso that he would receive a £4,000 payment in return when the young man inherited.

Of course, the Ardlamont purchase never really got off the ground, but it allowed Monson, presumably with Tottenham's advice, to begin searching out life insurance. He had attempted to insure Cecil back in 1892 for £15,000 but had been unsuccessful. Now, able to use the prospect of Ardlamont ownership as security, he went for £50,000. Scottish Provident turned him down, but London, Liverpool and Globe in Leeds were prepared to consider. He met with their Leeds manager, James Wardle, and set the terms. These simply stated that the beneficiary of the policy was to be his wife, Agnes. She, he told the insurers, had maintained Cecil for some four years and had incurred liabilities which were to be repaid upon his death. They hesitated and asked for more information. Monson then cancelled his proposal on 31 July and replaced it with a request for a smaller amount, £26,000, with an additional £22,000 to be added on one year later. The insurers declined, but this did not deter Monson. He adjusted the amount and finally secured two life insurance policies with Mutual Life, New York, for £10,000 each, again with Agnes as the beneficiary. It was these policies that eventually brought the police to his door.

With the death occurring in Scotland, there was no coroner's inquest. Instead, the decision as to accidental death or otherwise rested with the Procurator Fiscal. In this case, as was usual, he had received a report from the examining doctor, MacMillan, who was satisfied that death had been caused accidentally, and his own enquiries had raised no suspicions. Then Monson arrived at his door to inform him of the two life insurance policies. Up to that point, the Procurator Fiscal had been under the misapprehension that no life insurance existed. Discovering that Cecil Hambrough had in fact taken out this insurance, and that Monson's wife was set to benefit, raised his suspicions. He immediately ordered further enquiries, including the exhumation of the body. On 29 August, Monson was taken into custody.

For the next three months extensive enquiries were made as to the veracity of Monson and Scott's version of events back in August. Doctor Henry Littlejohn, a police surgeon, was brought in to examine Cecil Hambrough's body. He in turn collaborated with his friend Joseph Bell. These two men's fame would grow over the years as being Arthur Conan Doyle's real life Sherlock Holmes and Dr Watson. Between them they built a murder case around Monson, examining the body, the guns and the place where the shot was supposedly fired, concluding that Hambrough's death could not have been accidental. Essentially, it was the work that Littlejohn and Bell carried out during these intervening months that brought Alfred Monson to trial for murder. Without their input it is perhaps doubtful the case would ever have reached a court.

However, when the court sat on 12 December 1893, before Lord Chief Justice Clerk, Lord Kinsburgh (John Hay Athole Macdonald), Monson stood in the dock alone. Scott had absconded. He had left Ardlamont on the day of the shooting and subsequent enquiries had failed to find him. What had been uncovered was that his name was not Edward Scott. Police believed he was either Edward Sweeney or Ted Davis, and had been working as a bookmaker. When the charge was read to the court it applied to both men, though from the outset it is questionable just how involved Scott/ Sweeney/Davis could have been.

Monson, standing alone, was therefore on trial for attempted murder by drowning and actual murder by shooting. The drowning element of the charge came about after close examination of the first boat Monson and Hambrough had used on the fishing expedition revealed a hole had been made in the side of the vessel. This would, of course, have allowed water into the boat, which in turn would have made it eventually sink. However, this was a contentious issue from the start. Both boats used by Monson had plug holes already in the boat. These were designed to allow a small amount of water in but intended as an aid to remove water after the fishing had concluded. Splash fishing by its very nature involved splashing water vigorously to frighten the fish, a consequence of which was that water would inevitably be brought into the bottom of the boat. Various witnesses were brought to court to testify that the holes found by police had been crudely made and were unnecessary. But no evidence was produced that could show it was Monson who had made them. Doubt was also cast on his version of striking rocks and Hambrough clambering on to them after the sinking, after locals testified to there being no rocks to strike. But there was no proof.

It was the shooting incident that proved the most controversial and bizarre. To refute the notion that Hambrough had shot himself accidentally, Edinburgh gunsmith James MacNaughton had been taken to the Ardlamont estate whilst Monson was incarcerated. He was given the task of examining the site of the shooting and ascertaining whether or not, in his expert opinion, the young lieutenant had been responsible for his own death. MacNaughton was taken to where Cecil Hambrough was believed to be standing when the fatal shot was fired, and he began a reasonably forensic examination of the area around it. Knowing the wound that did the damage had been behind Hambrough's right ear and had taken away part of the middle of that ear, he was able to calculate that the shot had travelled from his left. Instructing a policeman of the same height to stand in the same spot allowed him to calculate a rough angle of shot. In direct line of sight was a rowan tree. Upon examination of that tree he found pellets had penetrated the trunk, broken smaller branches and punctured a number of leaves. Trees to the right of the rowan also showed pellet damage. Using tape measures, he ran a line back from each tree to where the policeman stood and beyond. Where they crossed, he calculated, was where the gun had been when the shot was fired.

Hambrough, he claimed, was killed by a shot fired approximately 9ft away, from behind him and to his left.

Doctor Littlejohn, who had carried out a full post-mortem on the exhumed body, concurred. In over two hours of evidence, Littlejohn was also adamant that Hambrough could not have killed himself. The wound, he testified, could not have been caused by a shot fired from behind in an upwards direction or from either the side or front. It had to have been fired from a distance of more than 3ft and less than 15ft, with 9ft being the most likely option. Of the wound itself, the fact that only four pellets from a cartridge that had contained 250–300 pellets had hit the skull, and no other pellets hit the body, was, he claimed, indicative of a glancing shot, fired from behind the lieutenant and at an angle that suggested the shooter was standing. These conclusions were based upon medical examination, the gunsmith's own calculations and firing a shotgun at human corpses, placed in various positions at Edinburgh's mortuary (something that would never be done today).

On the face of it, this was damning evidence and pointed an accusing finger in Monson's direction. But as the trial continued, its impact was blunted by testimony from various witnesses disputing the site of Hambrough's death. The body, as was constantly pointed out by Monson's defence, had also been moved, washed, dressed and buried. So whatever evidence had existed at the time of death had been compromised by all these events, plus natural decay, and if exactly where he had been found was unsubstantiated, then whatever was produced by experts had to be circumstantial at best.

When the judge made his summing up to the jury ten days after the start of the trial, it is probably fair to say he leaned more towards Monson's innocence than his guilt. Nothing had been proven, no guilt shown by the evidence presented, and much had been conjecture. The jury obviously agreed, in part, but doubt must have existed in their minds as they debated in the jury room before finally returning to the courtroom with a 'not proven' verdict.

This was no doubt a great relief for Monson, who walked away a free man, though it did nothing to enhance his reputation. He was shown to have been both scheming and unscrupulous in his dealings with Cecil Hambrough. Rebuilding his life after being exposed so publicly in a trial that had seen widespread publicity was never going to be easy, and so it proved. As for Scott – or Sweeney, or Davis – he did eventually surface, claiming innocence in the whole affair and talking up his great escape from justice to any who would listen, then faded back into obscurity.

So who did kill Cecil Hambrough? The evidence produced in court by both Doctor Littlejohn and the gunsmith, MacNaughton, seems to me to have the ring of truth about it. But I tend to lean toward it being an accident. Mystery man Scott, it later transpired had not been brought to Ardlamont to pose as an engineer intending to examine a yacht that Hambrough could not afford to buy, but because he was a bookmaker. Along with the property, Monson had purchased the shooting rights and those rights were worth money, particularly when organized shooting parties could be brought to the estate, pay fees to shoot and bet against each other using Scott's turf accountant skills. If that were the case, why murder Hambrough? It gained nothing and lost everything. As for the insurance policies, they are incriminating certainly, but Hambrough had only the best part of a year to wait before he reached 21 and their values could legally be obtained upon death. Killing him in 1893, almost a year before any legitimate claim could be made, makes little sense.

The case was never reinvestigated and, of course, remains unsolved.

*Chapter 4*

# The Baby Killer

*The murder of Rees Thomas Yells Brandish, 1897*

Elizabeth Brandish is believed to have been born in Little Compton, south Warwickshire, in 1864. Her parents eventually took over the licence to run the village's only public house, the Red Lion. It was a place Elizabeth grew up to know well, helping in the bar as a young woman before eventually moving away to work in a hotel in Gloucestershire. This was rural in location, busy much of the year round and, by all accounts, a place where she had intended to stay. But at some point in the early part of 1894, probably through her work in the hotel, she met and began an illicit affair with a wealthy local farmer. He was married, with a family of his own, so their meetings were clandestine and their association was never openly discussed, and would never offer the prospect of a future together. The affair quickly fell apart when she became pregnant that summer.

Alone and without support, Elizabeth suddenly found herself in a life-changing situation; the stigma of being pregnant outside of marriage would be corrosive both to herself and any family offering succour. So probably with that in mind, her family were never told, and she moved to Aldington, Kent, in early 1895. Friend Harriett Martin, who was aware of Elizabeth's dilemma, had offered her somewhere to stay during her confinement. Sensitive to her situation, Harriett had also written to Elizabeth prior to her arrival, offering a longer-term solution. Living close by, according to her letter, was an elderly couple, the Posts. They shared their home at Wye with their niece, Elizabeth Urben, who would take on the day-to-day care of Elizabeth's baby for a weekly allowance if she was willing to pay. This was by no means an unusual arrangement at this time, as many single women were forced to give up a child after birth or pay for ongoing nursing care if they could fund it. In the latter event, illegitimacy was often not declared, as was the case with Elizabeth Brandish. She agreed to the Post family taking the child but not to admitting that she was unmarried. So after giving birth to a boy in April or May 1895, whom she named Rees Brandish, she met with the Posts, using the alias of Mrs Edwards. The child at that stage was nine weeks old. Between them they agreed a weekly fee of five shillings (25p) to be paid monthly in advance by post. Any correspondence in return was to be addressed to The Red Lion, Little Compton. As far as Elizabeth Brandish was concerned, at that stage I would doubt she had any intention of ever seeing the child again. When she left Kent in late July that year, her problem had been solved and no-one need ever know.

A year or so after what must have been a traumatic experience, she joined the District Nursing Association at Clent, Worcestershire, an organization responsible for employing district nurses around the county and outlying areas and paying their wages. Often affiliated to the Queen's Nursing Institute, supported by Queen Victoria, these Associations offered security and a guaranteed level of income. For Elizabeth, it was a positive move and ensured payments to Kent would be maintained without too much financial hardship. Clearly her life had moved on, any damage to her reputation had been restored and a new future was within reach. Then she met Robert Narramore, a sergeant in the Worcestershire constabulary.

The two met when Elizabeth had been sent to his home in Clent to nurse his wife and daughter. Their association was initially based on no more than a passing acquaintance, any relationship being on a purely professional level. Then Narramore's wife died of pneumonia and things began to change. A welcome visitor to the house throughout their mother's illness, the sergeant's two daughters always felt comfortable in Elizabeth's company, as did he. She was reluctant to lose contact after the death, and had started to visit the family socially. That had eventually forged closer ties and led to her and the sergeant meeting together privately. Elizabeth even moved to lodgings in Clent, which aided both her district nursing work and her involvement with Narramore and his family. By the spring of 1897, so strong had the bonds between them become that it seems Elizabeth began to harbour thoughts of marriage, a prospect she was all too keen to embrace, but only if she felt confident that the secret of her son would never be uncovered. Something had to be done about Rees.

On 14 July, she wrote to Mrs Post enclosing £1 in payment for the coming month and informed her that it was her intention to take her son back in September. She gave as her reason a recent involvement with her sister in a small, undefined business venture, which would allow her to look after Rees on a full-time basis. The Posts were understandably upset. By this time they had been taking care of the little boy for just over two years, Elizabeth Urben the only mother he had ever known. Handing him back would be a wrench, though they never raised any serious objection and probably accepted that from the outset it had always been a financial arrangement, all too well aware that at some point there had always been the prospect of it coming to an end.

On 31 August, Elizabeth Brandish took a holiday from work and travelled over to see her brother at Drybank Farm, Ettington (6 miles south of Stratford). It was a yearly event, a summer holiday. She stayed there for just over a week and left by train on 8 September for Wye, the first time she had returned to see her son since leaving him behind in 1895. When she arrived at the Posts' house she had no luggage, only a small parcel and a length of what was described as 'Mackintosh material' (waterproof cloth), and wore her nurse's uniform. On the badge pinned to her cloak, whether by error or intention, was her name, 'E. BRANDISH'. The Post family took note. It was the first time they had realized that the name of Edwards was bogus. But they never challenged it. Perhaps it confirmed any suspicions they might have harboured about the woman they had only met once and needed no further explanation. They invited her to stay; they wanted to hold onto little Rees as long as they could. Elizabeth had no objections. Over tea, she explained that she was initially taking the boy to her brother's house at Ettington. There, he could mix with other children and be easily absorbed into the family. She also wanted to travel into Ashford before she returned, so a stay-over of two nights was agreed.

Elizabeth took a train into Ashford the following morning. There, she bought a large, lockable, tin bonnet box, along with a padlock, from High Street firm Lee & Sons, who specialized in various types of hat box. She then took the box to Ashford railway station and arranged for it to be held there until her return the following day. She told Elizabeth Urben upon her return what she had done, though never explained the rationale behind it. There followed some debate about the amount of luggage she would need for her journey home. Rees had clothes to pack, toys and of course a pram. These would be needed, at least Mrs Post thought so, and she organized the packing up of various items. But Elizabeth was adamant nothing was travelling back with her. The clothes, she argued, could stay in Wye and the pram and anything else too bulky should be forwarded on at a later date. Mrs Post thought that unfair. She wanted Rees to be surrounded by the things he knew and was familiar with. But Elizabeth remained resolute. The bulky items stayed, but not the boy's clothes. These, Mrs Post insisted, had to travel with them and she bundled them into a small parcel and forced Elizabeth to accept them.

Elizabeth left for Ettington on 10 September, the clothes wrapped in the mackintosh material. Elizabeth Urben accompanied them as far as the railway station, where Brandish collected her tin box, and watched as she carried it and the clothes onto the train. The little boy, smartly turned out in a dark blue coat with pearl buttons and a straw hat, waved goodbye to the woman he thought was his mother and the pair travelled on to London.

They arrived in the capital at five o'clock in the afternoon. For some never explained reason, they did not board a connecting train that night, whether by accident or intention is not known. Elizabeth was later found in the street, drunk on brandy, with the boy in tow. Local woman Ada Turner, who initially thought something amiss when she first saw them, put them in a cab and sent them off to Albany Road police station. There, the desk duty sergeant, Ralph Cockshaw, took them in and passed them over to the divisional police surgeon, who gave them both a thorough examination and found the boy had been sick but was otherwise well. Elizabeth Brandish, dressed in her district nurse's uniform, without her name badge, and using the name Edwards again, was clearly intoxicated, which she claimed had come about because the brandy she had consumed had been too strong. The surgeon, all too familiar with over-indulgence, held on to the pair for an hour or so, then had them escorted back to the railway station and placed on a train to Bletchley, which he understood to have been the intended destination. A more-sober nurse arrived there around 8.00 pm and booked herself and Rees into Bletchley's Station Hotel.

The following morning, the two of them were up early and back at the railway station by 8.00 am. There, Elizabeth bought third-class tickets to Stratford-upon-Avon and they boarded the 8.20 am train, which suggests Drybank Farm really was her intended destination. However, she obviously harboured doubts of some sort, borne out by the fact that at Blisworth, where she needed to change trains, she purposely delayed. The journey there had only taken forty minutes, and her connection was standing at a nearby platform with Stratford only one-and-a-half hours away. But perhaps in her mind, things were happening too fast. She needed time, so the connecting train left without them. In fact, she deliberately missed more than one connection, not leaving Blisworth until around 4.00 pm that afternoon. Where she went or what she did throughout that time is not known. What is known is that by half past four she was on the platform at Towcester station in Northamptonshire, where she needed to make a second change. There, she upgraded her ticket from third-class to second and again purposely delayed for almost three hours, pacing around the station trying to placate

Rees, who by this time was tired, understandably fretful and becoming ever more demanding. Station master James Owen remarked later that it was the little boy who had drawn his attention to the pair, so much so that he eventually helped put them both on the 7.19 train to Stratford and told the travelling guard, John Days, to keep an eye on them, which he did by leaving the train at Blakesley to look in through the compartment's window as the train stood for a few minutes at the platform. According to later testimony, mother and son were seated opposite each other at that stage and there was nothing to cause him any concern. There were no other passengers sharing the compartment. He checked again at Kineton. But by that time, around 8.15 pm, it was dark outside and Elizabeth had pulled down the blinds. There was nothing to see, but he recalled that he heard no noise. Ten minutes later, the train pulled into the station at Ettington. Days then went to help her out of the carriage. She was carrying what he thought was some sort of mackintosh and had an oval tin box, which was light enough for him to easily lift down. He had forgotten about the little boy.

Alone, Elizabeth walked from the train to the waiting room. There she sat quietly, her nurse's cloak around her, placed the tin trunk on the floor and held the mackintosh over her right arm. Porter William Hooten thought initially she was carrying a baby. The waiting room was somewhat dark and gloomy, so he waited until she walked back out onto the platform before asking for her ticket, which she handed over and at the same time asked if the bonnet box could be carried up to Drybank Farm that night. He explained that nothing could be done until morning, which was obviously no good for Elizabeth, but she raised no objection and carried it off herself. Half an hour later, having walked as far as the Ettington to Warwick crossroads, she plonked herself down on a bench, where local carrier John Heritage, returning by cart from Warwick, found her just after 9.00 pm and offered to take her up to Drybank after completing his delivery round in Ettington. Elizabeth gratefully accepted. His was a familiar face, and according to his later story she did not seem in any great hurry. He loaded the bonnet box, which was heavy, on to the back of the cart and she climbed up beside him, clutching a small brown paper parcel. The journey around the village took the best part of an hour, and she eventually arrived and knocked on the door at Drybank Farm a little after ten o'clock.

Sister-in-law Louisa, who had expected her back at some point earlier in the day, let her in and the carrier helped with the bonnet box. No-one seemed put out by the lateness of the hour. Elizabeth had been a regular visitor, and it appears no-one asked any awkward questions regarding her journey or her reasons for making it. The Brandishes had no doubt simply presumed it had been caused by either work or friends, and of course she was still on holiday. The secret of Rees had never been divulged, at least not to brother George. However, it transpired later that Louisa had been told by Elizabeth six months after the birth and sworn to secrecy. She had known of the boy's existence, but never his location. That secret Elizabeth had always held close, and there had been no further discussion about the boy in the year or so that followed his birth. As far as they were concerned, Elizabeth lived an independent life and nothing they had seen since her initial arrival a week or so earlier suggested there was anything to be concerned over. It was late, everyone wanted to be in their beds and Elizabeth had her own room upstairs. After a welcome hug and maybe a cup of tea, Elizabeth grabbed the tin box and carried it up to her bedroom.

The next morning, Sunday, Louisa went up to ask how long she planned to stay. She found Elizabeth packing clothes into a large trunk, owned by her and used months earlier to ferry belongings to and from the various locations Elizabeth had occupied around the county. It had eventually been relegated to the attic and brought back down from the roof space at Elizabeth's request whilst she had been away. Aware of her involvement with Sergeant Narramore and the recent move into Harriett Shilvock's lodging house at Clent, Louisa simply presumed taking more clothes was an indication that the relationship had an air of permanency about it, so never questioned it, nor the reason for the tin bonnet box to be packed in alongside it.

By 5.00 pm the following day, Elizabeth was back at the Narramore house, where she had been invited to spend the night, and the trunk was in the bedroom of her lodgings in Clent. Three days later, without any explanation, she and the large trunk containing that bonnet box were back at Drybank Farm. According to Louisa, she claimed to have been visiting a friend in Birmingham. This time the large trunk, unopened, stayed in the kitchen and she left for Clent after two days. For a few weeks life went on as normal. Elizabeth returned to her nursing care duties and tended patients in and around Clent. Marriage to the police sergeant began to look ever more likely, and with the issue of having to pay fees for child care to the Post family ended, she felt the future had prospects she could at last take advantage of. But the Posts had not gone away; they had a forwarding address at Little Compton, and they used it. After taking care of Rees for almost two-and-a-half years, there was an attachment they could not shake off, nor wanted to. They needed reassurance that he was well and being cared for as he should be. They wrote within days of Rees being taken away to arrange for his pram to be sent on to where ever Elizabeth was living. There were costs involved and they expected the nurse to send money to facilitate the pram being sent by train. Elizabeth ignored the letter. Elizabeth Urben, concerned over this lack of response, wrote again: 'I was looking out anxiously for the letter to know how my little darling was getting on, bless him. I am always thinking of him day and night … I wish I lived nearer to you, then I could run in and see him, but it takes 26 shillings from here.'

It made little difference: the letter was again ignored. The Posts, by now seriously concerned, wrote to Ettington's vicar, believing Elizabeth to have been a church-going woman. Surely he would have seen the little boy. He had not, but he knew the Brandish family and Elizabeth the district nurse. Whether through him or through the Post family, that lack of confirmation of the boy's presence in Ettington eventually brought in the police. Their enquiries were initially kept low key, secrecy being closely maintained as they sifted the known facts. But by 18 October, Superintendent Alfred Pugh of Worcestershire police, satisfied that Rees Brandish really had disappeared and of Elizabeth Brandish's involvement, opened out the investigation and interviewed Robert Narramore. He in turn confronted Elizabeth that same night. She confessed to being the mother of the little boy, but insisted he was not missing but in the care of a woman who had wanted to adopt him. Unfortunately, she had no details of just who this woman was, where she lived, whether single or married or what her name was. But this was 1897, and as a policeman he had come across desperate single mothers before. What may seem preposterous today was obviously less so at that time. The stigma and scandal brought to the door of any woman in such a situation often led to desperate acts. Narramore accepted her story and the couple's relationship held. Four days later, Superintendent Pugh, after receiving instructions from Ashford police, travelled to Clent to Harriett Shilvock's home and interviewed Elizabeth Brandish as to the whereabouts of her son. She told him the same story:

'I met a woman on Clent Hill this summer, not long before I went away at the beginning of September and was talking about children. Some had them that did not want them. She said she would like to adopt one. I said I knew of one, and that I could get it for her. She agreed to take it, but no-one was to know anything about it. I saw her several times … she went to Ashford in the same train, but not the same carriage. I went to Wye and she stayed in Ashford. The next day I went to Ashford and saw her again. While in Ashford

I bought a tin box. We came to London, but the woman would not take it that day ... I saw her at Towcester and she told me to get into another compartment, and she took the child. Then I went on to my brother at Ettington.'

Pugh accepted the story at face value and went away to begin a search around the Birmingham area. Back at Clent, the relationship still held and a week later Elizabeth arrived at Narramore's house with an oval tin bonnet box. She told him she had washed some clothes in it and had caused a little rust. She wanted him to paint the inside, which he did. But the superintendent and his police team had not gone away. Convinced, after his enquiries had failed to find the woman whom Elizabeth had insisted had taken the boy, that there was far more to the disappearance of Rees Brandish than they had at first believed, he widened the investigation, shifting its emphasis from that of a missing child to that of a murdered child. In turn that led to Elizabeth Brandish being formally arrested on 9 November, which allowed them to widen the scope of their enquiries even further and gave them cause to descend on Drybank Farm. If Rees was dead, then he had to be there. On 13 November, it seemed they were vindicated when the body of a small boy was found buried beneath cabbages.

From the moment of its discovery, police were convinced the body was that of Rees Brandish. Their enquiries had by this time been ongoing for almost a month. Elizabeth Brandish's movements over the end of August and through September were successfully mapped, and countless potential witnesses on the railways who had seen her travel to and from Kent were interviewed. This had allowed the police to plot her movements over the crucial days highlighted by Elizabeth Urben and the Post family. The interview with the district nurse in October essentially corroborated the Post family's suspicions regarding Rees. The story concocted by Elizabeth Brandish about the boy being adopted by a stranger from Birmingham was never believed. Follow-up enquiries failed to add any credible supporting evidence; and what of that tin bonnet box? Questioning of railway staff had apparently already underlined its importance. Everyone interviewed recalled seeing it. They had found the shop where the purchase had been made, and noted the change in its weight when carried. In turn, that had led to the belief that the boy could have been murdered, placed inside this oval box with its internal lock and external padlock, and carried away from Ettington railway station. So the body in the cabbage patch could not be anyone else, could it?

Today this would be an open and shut case. DNA evidence alone would solve the problem of the body's identity. But obviously in 1897 that science had not yet been discovered, which was going to make this extremely difficult to confirm. The body, which had been placed in the ground in a foetal position, lying on its right side, had been covered over in lime. It was naked, but the lime had destroyed the facial features. Easy identification was therefore not possible.

At the inquest, held at the Chequers Inn, Ettington, two days later, Doctor William Fenton, Kineton's only doctor, gave the coroner his initial results. According to his testimony, the body found was that of a boy, aged around 2½ years-old, 34in (0.86m) tall, with light brown hair. In an advanced state of decomposition, the body had been in the ground for about two months, but the teeth were still intact and numbered sixteen, eight in each jaw. There was staining of the subcutaneous tissue at the front of the neck and upper chest, which he believed had been caused by pressure being applied in life. In other words, the boy had probably been strangled. Death, he believed, would have taken three to four minutes. He added that police had retrieved a sample of the boy's hair from the Post family. Elizabeth Urben had retained, as a keepsake, pieces of hair after she had cut the boy's hair. It was being examined by experts looking to ascertain a match with the body, but results were not known at that stage.

Circumstantial though this evidence was, it damned Elizabeth Brandish. The body matched Rees Brandish's age, his height and his hair colour, and had been buried around the time of his known disappearance from the Towcester to Ettington train. As far as police were concerned, it had to be the missing boy and his killer had to have been his mother. However, the inquest needed more, and adjourned for a month. It resumed on 15 December at Ettington's Reading Rooms. Doctor Stevenson, lecturer on forensic medicine at Guy's Hospital in London and the Home Office's scientific analyst, was the key witness. He had concluded his examination of the body and was able to confirm to the coroner that no poison had been used. There had been no infection in the lungs, and the hair supplied by Elizabeth Urben was in all probability a match for that found on the boy's body. Other witnesses testified as to Elizabeth Brandish's movements on the key days, and the jury, after thirty-five minutes of consultation, returned a verdict of 'wilful murder' against her and accepted the body discovered as that of Rees Brandish. Twenty-four hours later, the magistrates' court returned the same verdict and the nurse was sent back to prison to await her trial at the Warwick Assizes.

On the face of it, the case had been solved. But ridiculous as it may seem, the evidence was not really strong enough and all of it circumstantial. The body in the ground could not, satisfactorily, be identified as being the missing boy. No-one actually saw her carry out the murder. The boy could have left the Stratford train without being seen before it arrived at Ettington. The guard supposedly keeping an eye on the woman and her son had not even realized that when she left the train for the last time, the little boy had not been with her. Even the hair, scientifically examined, could not be definitively identified as being from the body in the ground. The case was thus high on speculation and low on actual evidence, and Elizabeth Brandish refused to admit any guilt.

The trial opened in March 1898 before Lord Russell. Public interest was such that huge crowds, the majority of them women, descended on Warwick's Shire Hall in the hope of gaining access to the public gallery. Long queues had formed in the streets outside by the time the doors opened. Most were unsuccessful, the hall only having seating for around forty or fifty people. Even the press, who had turned up in overwhelming numbers, had difficulty finding seats. What space that was available was allocated mainly to local newsmen and those from Birmingham.

In essence, the prosecution's case, led by Mr J.S. Dugdale QC, was straightforward enough. Little had changed, in their view, from the evidence presented in the magistrates' court. Rees Brandish had died on the train journey back to Ettington, his body then being placed inside the tin bonnet box and carried to Drybank Farm. From there it had been taken to Clent, the intention being to bury him in Mrs Shilvock's garden. But when the larger trunk containing clothes and the bonnet box had arrived in Clent, Elizabeth Brandish had not been at home. A neighbour took the box in, and she and Mrs Shilvock had carried it up to the nurse's bedroom. That, according to the Crown, had been enough to prevent her taking the body out into the back garden. The same large trunk, along with the bonnet box, had been taken back to Drybank. There, it had remained downstairs, which had facilitated her in taking the body outside unseen. There, she had stripped it, buried it in a 1ft-deep hole and covered it in lime. The ground was used later for growing cabbages.

Much of this made sense, though to postulate that Elizabeth had carried the body between her brother's house and her own lodgings in reasonably warm weather was a relatively new theory, brought about after police had carried out door-to-door enquiries around Harriett Shilvock's home. These revealed that Elizabeth Brandish built a fire in her back garden at a time her landlady was known to be away, and in the same week of the boy's disappearance. The remnants of that fire had remained in the garden. Sifting the ashes revealed a single pearl button. The button, they believed, came from the coat worn by Rees Brandish. If she had burnt his clothing, it suggested she had carried the body back to Clent, stripped it there and destroyed the evidence outside before returning to Ettington to bury it.

The only other key piece of evidence was a letter. When Elizabeth Brandish was arrested on 9 November, she had in her possession a letter she intended to post on to Sergeant Narramore. The letter was a rambling affair about her state of mind at that time, reflecting on her previous interview with Superintendent Pugh and the investigation she was aware was taking place in Ettington. But the significant lines are as follows: 'My one great trouble is that my dearest brother and family may be brought into trouble through me.'

At the time this letter was written, no search had been mounted in the garden of Drybank Farm and the only person who could have known about the body and the trouble its discovery would bring to the Brandish family was Elizabeth. As far as the Crown was concerned, this was proof positive she had put the boy's body in the ground, and if she had done that then she had murdered him.

The problem for the prosecution, regardless of how damning all this was for Elizabeth Brandish, was the jury. At the end of the trial, having listened to all this and the conclusive evidence of her illegitimate child being fostered then taken by her from Wye, they could not agree. According to later newspaper interviews, one particular member of that jury, George Euston, had refused from the outset to accept the argument that the prosecution had produced enough evidence to show the body found was actually that of Rees Brandish. Nor had they been able to show murder had taken place on the train and that the body, 34in in length, had been ferried around Warwickshire in a tin bonnet box. Of course, he was right. Everything produced in the courtroom had been based upon circumstantial evidence; though, it has to be said, somewhat overwhelming circumstantial evidence. It transpired later that, whilst these were all valid arguments in favour of his viewpoint, his real objection had been over the use of capital punishment. So, the trial ended with a jury in dispute and a retrial set for later in the year.

This second trial took place at the end of July, this time before Mr Justice Darling. Never likely to prove a successful prosecution for the Crown, the case had been examined thoroughly by the press, as had the jury's indecision in March. Nothing new emerged, and after three days Elizabeth Brandish was declared not guilty and released. For many in that courtroom, when the verdict was finally announced, justice had not been done, and the reception by those in the public gallery was mainly hostile. So to this day the case remains unsolved.

Did Elizabeth Brandish do it? On the evidence available, it has to seem likely. As the judge said to the jury in her second trial:

> 'If the body found was not the prisoner's child it was someone else's. How did it get there? Who had an interest in putting it there? If it were anyone else's child had anyone else in the neighbourhood lost one? Prisoner had a child of that age, sex, colour. It had never been seen since 11 September last year. … If it were not her child, was it not an extraordinary coincidence that she lost a child of that sort in the neighbourhood, and that it was just such a child as was found in the garden of her brother?'

*Above left*: Madeleine Smith as she appeared at her trial for the murder of Pierre Emile L'Angelier. (*Mary Evans Picture Library*)

*Above right*: Pierre L'Angelier's lodging house.

The Gare Loch, which was overlooked by the Smith family's summer house.

THE PRISONER, JOHN MONSON

LIEUTENANT HAMBROUGH
Shot in a wood near Ardlamont House in August
last. From a Photograph by M. Asquith, Harrogate

EDWARD "SCOTT"
The man who is "wanted." From an auth
Photograph

*Above*: Images of the three men at the centre of the Ardlamont murder. Published by *The Graphic*. (*Mary Evans Picture Library*)

*Left*: Tighnabruaich and Ardlamont Point.

Providence house, Peasenhall. Rose Harsent had a room on the top floor.

Ipswich County Hall where Gardiner's trial took place. (*Suffolk Record Office*)

*Above left*: Rose Harsent. (*Suffolk Record Office*)

*Above right*: A newspaper image of Emily Dimmock. (© *The British Library Board/ British Newspaper Archive*)

Sir Edward Marshall Hall, who defended both Robert Wood in 1907 and Harold Greenwood in 1920.

# The Trial of Robert Wood : At the New Bailey

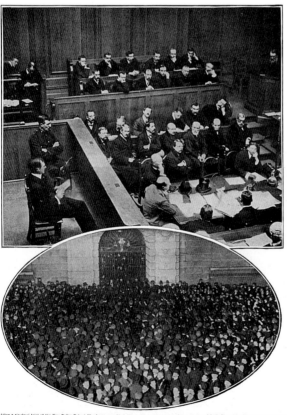

After a six-days' trial at the New Bailey Robert Wood was acquitted, late on Wednesday night, of the murder of Emily Dimmock. The result was cheered by thousands of people who had been waiting outside the court for hours. At the top is a photograph of the court when Wood's father gave evidence. Below is a flashlight photograph of the crowd taken directly after the verdict was known

The trial of Robert Wood. He was charged with murdering prostitute Emily Dimmock in what became known as the Camden Town Murder. (© *Illustrated London News Ltd./Mary Evans*)

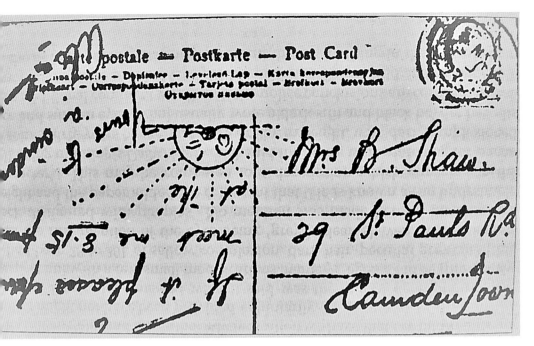

The Rising Sun postcard sent to Emily Dimmock by Robert Wood.

Ightham village, Kent, as it looked at the start of the twentieth century.

Ightham village church, where Caroline Luard was buried.

*Above left*: Harold Greenwood.

*Above right*: Mable Greenwood. (*Alamy*)

Rumsey House.

Kineton railway station, where it is thought Elizabeth Brandon murdered her child as the train stood on the platform. (*Warwickshire County Records Office*)

*Right*: Line drawing of the discovery of Florence Nightingale Shore.

*Below*: Ettington Village as Elizabeth Brandish would have known it.

The Percy Arms, Otterburn.

Otterburn as it looked in the 1930s.

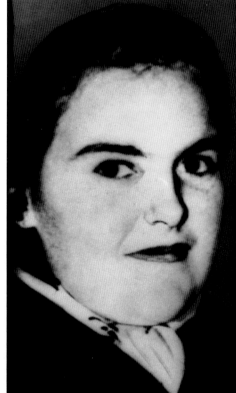

*Above left*: The house at Ashton where the bodies of George and Lillian Peach where discovered.

*Above right*: Ann Noblett. (*Alamy*)

*Chapter 5*

# The Peasenhall Mystery

*The murder of Rose Harsent, 1902*

Early on the morning of 1 June 1902, William Harsent pushed through the gate of Providence House, an old, large house in the Suffolk village of Peasenhall, and made his way up the narrow path carrying fresh linen for his daughter, Rose. A live-in domestic servant to local Baptist elder William Crisp and his wife, Georgiana, she had a room above the kitchen, which had its own door at the back of the house. Her day should have already begun, this being Monday morning, so he probably fully expected the kettle to be on the hob and tea already in the pot. Such was the pattern of life in service he had become familiar with since his daughter had moved into the Crisp's home. But this was to be no ordinary morning. The house was quiet. The kitchen window had been covered over to shut out the light – not something Rose usually did – which meant the room itself was dark, suggesting she had overslept. But bizarrely, when he tried the door it was unlocked.

Rose Harsent lay on her back on the kitchen floor. Clearly dead, her throat had been cut and her nightdress had been burned away. The floor and much of her body was awash with blood. Faced with this unimaginable horror, and no doubt in shock, William's reaction is perhaps understandable. He threw the kitchen rug over her and left. There was nothing else to be done. Outside, he found neighbours and they, in turn, found local police constable Eli Nunn. It is his record of what he found in Providence House that has mystified and confounded ever since.

Rose Harsent lived in a self-contained bedroom. It was reached by its own staircase that ran from the kitchen, which had been built on to the back of the house along with a small conservatory, up to the house's top floor. A short corridor then ran on to her room. In the kitchen itself, which measured approximately 10ft x 8ft (3.04m x 2.44m), was an internal door that led to other parts of the house and a back door leading to the outside.

This meant when the inner door was closed, which it was at night, Rose could entertain visitors unobserved by the house's owners, Mr and Mrs Crisp. According to PC Nunn, when he found her body that morning, Rose lay on the floor with her head resting on the staircase. Her throat had been cut from ear to ear, with blood splatter extending up the stairs and around her feet. A newspaper rested beneath her head, dated 30 May 1902. To one side of her body lay a candlestick and a burnt-out candle. To the other side was a kitchen lamp which had been taken to pieces. Not far from the body lay a broken medicine bottle, its cork stopper still wedged firmly into the bottle neck. A wall shelf near the outside door had been pulled down. It appeared she had been set alight after she had died. The newspaper was charred and the whole of the front of her nightdress was burnt away, leaving only material around her neck, which had caused extensive burning to her arms and torso, though her face and hair were virtually untouched. Strangely, she still wore her stockings. The table cloth covering the kitchen's table was also singed. Blood had pooled around her body. A woman's shawl, presumably Rose's, had been fastened up over the kitchen window. There was also a smell of paraffin about the room.

PC Nunn, after satisfying himself that nothing could be done for Rose, went upstairs to examine her room, where he found three letters, a copy of some obscene verses and a bed that had not been slept in. One of the letters, in a buff envelope, had arranged an appointment for the previous night: 'Dear R, I will try to see you tonight at 12 o'clock at your place. If you put a light in your window at ten for about ten minutes, then you can put it out again. Do not have a light in your room at 12 as I will come round the back way.'

It was unsigned, clearly of importance to police, and suggestive of an appointment that had been kept: either a meeting that went wrong or a meeting to murder. More correspondence, much of it mundane, was found in a further search made later in the day.

Doctor Charles Ley was called, arriving at Providence House at around 8.40 am. He confirmed death, but more importantly also examined the broken medicine bottle and discovered its label still partly attached; a label he recognized as his own and with the name of its intended recipients – the children of Mrs Gardiner, a neighbour – still legible. According to his later report, the bottle also had a smell of paraffin about it. So began the police investigation, based solely on Doctor Ley's supposition that this bottle's contents had caused the fire and the belief that someone in the Gardiner household was responsible.

The Gardiners, who lived some 200 yards away, were a family of eight. Married in 1888, they had lived in Peasenhall for twelve years and were extremely well regarded by all those who knew them. William Gardiner, the father and the man police believed from the outset had written the letter and committed the murder, was a devout, respectable Primitive Methodist and member of the nearby Sibton congregation; as was, it transpired later, Rose Harsent. By the end of Tuesday, 3 June, after local enquiries had suggested a promiscuous side to William's character, police wasted no time in making an arrest, his clothing and only pocket knife later seized for a rudimentary forensic examination.

Guilt, of course, would be determined by the results of that examination and whatever other evidence the police investigation could eventually place before a jury. At that point everything they had was purely circumstantial. All they really knew at this time was that in May 1901, William Gardiner had been implicated in an affair with Rose. A local scandal was brought about by two young men, George Wright and Alphonse Skinner, who claimed to have overheard the couple whilst they stood outside what was known as the Peasenhall Doctor's Chapel. Exactly what they heard has never really been clarified, but the pair certainly let it be known that whatever had happened inside was of a sexual nature. This had been enough in 1902 to cause Gardiner to lose his good name within the church and place a burden on Rose that she probably never deserved. Further enquiries produced evidence that Gardiner was in the habit of writing to her; at least two of his letters were found in her bedroom. It also appeared he had met with her on occasion during the past months. But it was the results of Doctor Ley's post-mortem that confirmed their suspicion and convinced them of the veracity of their case.

He carried out a full post-mortem on Rose on the same day as Gardiner's arrest. What he found was a deep, jagged cut across her neck, already noted by PC Nunn, which had severed the trachea and both internal jugular veins. There was a stab wound on the left side of her chest, a bruise to the right side of her face and jaw, along with defensive wounds found on both hands as if she had tried to prevent the knife attack. Those wounds, Doctor Ley confirmed, had not been self-inflicted. The charring to her body, which was significant, was nevertheless superficial and caused after death. There was no blistering which would have occurred had she still been alive when the fire started. More importantly for police, she was also six months pregnant at the time of her death. The motive for murder, in their opinion, had been found and the noose around Gardiner's neck began to tighten.

The contentious issues all surrounded the time of death. When Doctor Ley had first seen the body *in situ*, rigor mortis was evident in the upper part of her body. For him that placed death around four hours earlier, which would mean the killing took place about 4.00 am. After his post-mortem, he widened that time a little and placed her murder at some four to six hours earlier, which could have pushed it back to around 2.00 am. In many ways his post-mortem, whilst producing a clear motive, also muddied the waters as far as implicating their suspect went. Everything the police had surmised up to this point was based on the presumption that whoever wrote the letter setting up a midnight meeting, had to have been the killer. If that were true, why would he have waited for two hours before killing her? It was a question no doubt debated long into the night on more than one occasion. Understanding more about William Gardiner and his movements that night obviously became of paramount importance to the case.

According to Gardiner's wife, there was really nothing to find. She told police she had been aware of the accusations against her husband and Rose Harsent, but had never believed them to be true. There had been an enquiry into the alleged affair carried out on behalf of the chapel by Reverend John Guy, which had eventually exonerated him. The couple had discussed it, and Rose had continued to visit them at their cottage regardless of local gossip. They had known each other for over seven years, and as far as Mrs Gardiner was concerned, the claims made about there being a secret affair were nonsense; particularly an affair continuing long after the accusations were proved false.

Gardiner certainly had a lot to lose if they were proven to be true. Being employed as a foreman for local company Smyth & Sons for the past four or five years gave him a deal of credibility, as did his adherence to religious values and the responsibility of providing for six children. But lesser men have strayed, and the last person to know is usually the wife. So, regardless of Georgianna Gardiner's denial, the investigation continued to centre around him and his movements that night. The police believed she was wrong, and hoped at some point to uncover an opportunity for him to have left the house, crossed over to Providence House, had a clandestine meeting and then committed murder, and a pretty bloody one at that.

Exactly what he did that night was not too difficult to discover. There were enough witnesses to confirm his movements up until the early hours of 1 June. On the afternoon of 31 May he had been in Leiston and Kelsale, some 2 or 3 miles from the coast, with his daughter. He arrived back home by around 9.30 pm, when the couple had eaten a late meal. At around

10.00 pm he was standing in the street outside his front door – from where he could see Rose Harsent's bedroom window – talking to neighbour and local bricklayer Harry Burgess. The two of them had discussed the coming thunderstorm which could be seen gathering in the distance. Harry later confirmed that a light in Rose's window could clearly be seen at ten o'clock. Presumably, William had also noted it. As the storm began at around 11.30 pm, the Gardiners left their children in bed and paid a visit to next-door neighbour Rose Dickinson, who managed the local ironmongers shop, staying with her until the storm had begun to abate at around 1.30 am, when they returned home. He apparently slept through until around half past eight, whilst his wife had been up feeling unwell in the early hours and did not, according to her, return to bed until daylight (around 4.00 am). This was corroborated in part by the neighbour on the other side of their house, Amelia Pepper. She told police she had heard Mrs Gardiner get up at around 2.20 am. The walls between her bedroom and the Gardiners' were thin, and sounds of movement were easily distinguishable. Besides, she told them, Mrs Gardiner spoke, her familiar voice easily recognizable.

But none of this deflected police from their original hypothesis. To their minds, having concluded some exhaustive local enquiries – which included gamekeeper James Morris, who claimed to have seen a trail of 'footsteps' after the storm between Providence House and the Gardiners' cottage – William Gardiner, and only William Gardiner, could have murdered Rose Harsent. They brought the case to court on the grounds that he had been involved in an affair with the victim for more than a year, meeting secretly, possibly regularly, probably always as the 'Dear R' letter describes. Gardiner had then discovered, possibly early in 1902, he was the father of her unborn child and, cornered by the situation, had resorted to murder. The problem the police had was how to prove it.

After almost six months in prison, William Gardiner finally stood in the dock at the Suffolk Autumn Assizes in Ipswich before the Honourable Sir William Grantham Knight (Mr Justice Grantham) and pleaded 'not guilty' to murder. The story of the discovery of Rose Harsent's body was retold, Constable Nunn gave a long, precise and detailed explanation of the murder scene, doctors Charles Ley and John Richardson – both of whom had examined the body – recounted the autopsy findings, and numerous friends and neighbours testified as to the character and veracity of the accused man. The writer of the obscene letters and verses had by this time also been discovered. He was 20-year-old Frederick Davis, who lived next door to Rose. He admitted his involvement, and in testimony to the court claimed he had written them only after she had asked him to do so. Finally, and perhaps seen as most importantly, James Morris recounted his finding wet footprints, made by a rubber sole, in an almost direct line between Rose Harsent's kitchen and the Gardiner cottage. However, this information he had kept to himself initially, the police never able to verify its reliability. Other than that, there was little by way of new evidence. Writing experts were brought in to examine Gardiner's handwriting in order to ascertain whether or not he had written the letter requesting the midnight meeting. Some were categorical in their assertion he had been the author, but others less so. Forensic evidence was produced with regards to the clothing police had seized early in the investigation, but the examination had failed to find any blood staining, and the pocket knife had also proven to be clean. Even the type, texture and colour of envelopes found in Rose's room became a point of contention. Enquiries at the local post office had found the buff envelope PC Nunn discovered containing the 'Dear R' letter was delivered to Providence House on the afternoon of 31 May. Mrs Crisp had told police she had seen it herself, which corroborated the constable's belief that the letter and the envelope belonged together. This raised the question of whether Gardiner ever used or had access to that particular buff coloured envelope at home or at work? Testimony from a variety of witnesses suggested not.

All the prosecution were left with was the supposed affair and dalliance in the Doctor's Chapel in May 1901, and the broken medicine bottle. In the case of the former, despite close questioning of the two young men who spread the gossip, there was little proof. As for the bottle labelled for use by the Gardiner family, Georgianna Gardiner told the jury that she had once owned it and that it had contained camphorated oil, but she had given it to Rose Harsent not long after receiving it from the doctor for her to treat a cold. Ernest Wild, barrister for the defence, argued strongly that it was Rose herself who had then reused it to hold paraffin, which she poured over the fire coals each morning to help light the kitchen fire.

Confusion and doubt had thus been successfully sown, and by the time the trial reached its fourth day it's fair to say little concrete evidence had reached the courtroom. But there was still enough circumstantial evidence to convict if the jurors were so minded. Here, William Gardiner got lucky. After retiring to discuss their verdict at the conclusion of the judge's summing up, only one juror held out for a 'not guilty' verdict, but it was enough. The law demanded unanimity, and after learning of the jury's dilemma, the judge dismissed them and ordered a retrial. Gardiner lived to fight another day, returning to prison to rebuild his case for what would be his second murder trial.

The new trial began on 24 January 1903, by which time there was far less public hostility towards Gardiner. Opinion as to his guilt had changed during the two months of his continued incarceration. Funds had even been raised to help finance his legal costs, with money also donated to aid the supportive, but ever-more impoverished, Georgianna. The Harsent family, of course, still believed strongly in his guilt, as did some members of his church. But the notion that Rose had been leading a blameless life was questioned, and for the first time caused doubt to be expressed over Gardiner's involvement, as prosecutor Henry Dickens, son of the famous author Charles, was all too well aware. The growing national interest and questioning audit of his case was reported and discussed up and down the country by the time Dickens took his seat in the courthouse in Ipswich. What he needed was new evidence, but there was none.

There were three letters of confession, as often happens in murder cases, but none veracious enough to warrant close inspection and therefore of little use to Dickens, though he knew his adversary would use them to cause disquiet amongst the jurors, which he duly did. But, more importantly, no new prosecution witnesses had come forward to bolster the Crown's case and silence the dissenters. So when Dickens addressed the court, it was to present evidence that had remained unfettered and unaltered by time or opinion since the first trial, and it duly failed a second time. The jury, after four days, as had happened previously, was unable to reach a decision based on the evidence they had heard. Another retrial was ordered by the judge, with the date set for a possible June hearing and a change of venue to the Old Bailey in London.

It was a blow to the Gardiner team, who had probably fully expected a 'not guilty' verdict in light of how both press and public had supported their cause. Ernest Wild QC argued vociferously that there was now no point in taking the case forward a third time. The Crown tended to agree, and within days had entered a *nolle prosequi* into court, which meant no prosecution evidence would be submitted and Gardiner was released. The case was finally over. Nationally, the news was greeted with delight and approbation; in Peasenhall, with silence and regret. There would be no return to village life for the Gardiners and their family. For them it was a new life in South London, and hopefully obscurity. Ernest Wild remained a friend of the family for many years. Henry Dickens continued prosecuting cases in the Old Bailey until his retirement in 1932. This was without doubt, for both men, their most memorable case, and the fact it remained unsolved for the rest of their lives was a mixed blessing.

So, did William Gardiner murder Rose Harsent? Looking at the state of Rose Harsent's body with a modern eye, it appears to me that the doctor's time of death is wrong. Rigor mortis had set in on the upper body, but not the lower. That tends to suggest death could have occurred six or seven hours earlier. Doctor Ley saw Rose's body at around half past eight in the morning, which pushes death back to around 1.30 am at the earliest. We know exactly where Gardiner was at this time, and to believe he had committed murder means we also have to believe his wife was complicit. Besides, why would he write a letter, post it, set a time for the meeting and then, after murdering Rose, not take the letter back? It makes little sense to me, so I cannot accept that he was guilty and escaped justice.

My belief is that the murder remains unsolved because police only ever centred their enquiries on the one man. There are also other clues. In their book *The Peasenhall Murder*, Martin Fido and Keith Skinner examined the notion of a candle in the window as a signal to confirm a meeting. What they discovered was that to identify that signal, one needed to be close to Providence House. Rose always lit a candle when she went to bed, her room would always have shown light and Gardiner would have been able to see it. But he would not have been able to specifically distinguish a light in the room from a lighted candle in the window. In other words, the signal was more than useless if you couldn't be close enough to see the flame, and he was not. I agree with their findings. Besides, the writing of the appointment letter was never really seen as having been written by William Gardiner. Morris's claim of seeing footprints are pretty meaningless and could never be corroborated, so have to be discounted.

Clearly, someone entered that kitchen in the early hours of 1 June. Rose had blocked up the kitchen window and had waited upstairs, and her bed showed she had not slept in it. So, did her lover arrive and kill her? Quite probably, but the way her body was found suggests she never saw her killer. The kitchen door and entry into the conservatory were not barred, and the attack appears to have started whilst she was standing, the final attack made when she was on the ground. The candlestick found beside her suggests it was in her hand when she was struck and she was at the bottom of the stairs, which showed evidence of blood spatter on the bottom steps. Perhaps the medicine bottle was a red herring and the fire an attempt to hide something, though exactly what remains a mystery. But who killed her, and why?

Rose was six months pregnant, which could have been enough of a motive. Or she could have been murdered by a third party, someone she knew, someone she trusted. And why was neighbour Harry Burgess out on the street at that late hour?

## Chapter 6

# The Camden Town Murder

*The murder of Emily Dimmock, 1907*

Camden Town in 1907 had changed significantly from the leafy, middle-class suburb it had intended to be fifty years earlier. Then, its three-storey homes had housed moneyed families, whose wealth bought comfort and an army of domestic servants employed to maintain it. But those upwardly mobile families had slowly moved away. The family homes, lost through a lack of financial support, had been divided up into apartments and, over time, populated by boarders and lodgers. Another crowded London suburb had been born, although of itself that was no bad thing. Employment was plentiful. The LNWR railway was perhaps the biggest of an ever-widening group of firms providing jobs with its nearby goods yards, along with the town's own huge bakery, soft drinks factory and the piano-making industry, which took advantage of the canal system to carry in wood. In turn, that attracted the retail industry. A growing static workforce is needful, and business has a voracious appetite. Small shops and public houses quickly moved in, and following on behind came prostitution.

Emily Dimmock fell into the latter category. Born in rural Hertfordshire in 1884 and educated in Hitchin, Emily's early life was set to follow a path well worn by most women at that time: mundane work, routine marriage and over-large family. Her first paid job, working in a factory making straw hats in Luton, began the process. She was 15 years old. When her sister, Rebecca, moved to London to take on a domestic service role, the lure of the capital was stronger than that of a rural hat-maker. It took time, but eventually she followed, moving to East Finchley to take on the role of housemaid to a wealthy family. From that point on her life was going to follow a new and very different path, though not in service. Dissatisfaction with the job – or the hours, or perhaps the family who employed her – brought her back briefly to Luton when she was 20. There was even a short-lived return to making hats, but the work could not be guaranteed and quite probably London had offered another, more profitable way of earning a living. By the end of 1904, working as a prostitute, she was plying her trade along the Euston Road, and within a year she became a regular and popular face in the Rising Sun public house. Clearly successful, she had a number of regular paying clients, most of whom only knew her by her working name of 'Phyllis', and whose money allowed her to live independently. However, it obviously came with risks attached. Working as a prostitute, particularly one working regularly, meant contracting disease was almost inevitable. So it proved for Emily, syphilis taking her off the streets at one point during 1905.

Fortunately for her it was also a curable disease, and taking time out probably aided her recovery. What she did not do was change her lifestyle, even though it made her pause and reassess, as serious illness often does. Of necessity, perhaps, she took herself out of London and at some point later that year it is thought she met, possibly fell in love with and may even have married a young sailor based in Portsmouth. Her family certainly believed that to be the case and she actively promoted the idea of being a married woman, wearing and showing a ring on occasion, but she never allowed it to interfere with her work, which seems to have continued unabated. Sailors are often at sea, and being based in Portsmouth often put distance between them. The two were never able to meet for any length of time, a situation which may well have suited Emily.

Essentially the relationship, true or false, was doomed to failure, even though there seems to be some evidence suggestive of a real and deeply felt love affair. But Emily was clearly not going to turn her back on London, and slowly, over a period of perhaps 18 months, the sailor eventually disappeared from her life. He was replaced at some point in 1906 by a new man, Bertram Shaw, a cook working in restaurant cars for the Midland Railway. The two had met in the Rising Sun, and, after a courtship of sorts, moved in together in January 1907, with Emily calling herself Mrs Shaw from that point on whilst still maintaining a presence on the street as 'Phyllis'.

How much Shaw knew at this time of Emily's life as a working prostitute is debatable. But he cannot have lived alongside her in blissful ignorance. Twice that year they moved lodgings – the fact that Emily entertained men when he was not there was cited as the cause on at least one occasion – before finally ending up at 29 St Paul's Road in July. Their new landlady believed them to be married and was totally unaware of Emily's sexual proclivity. Discretion, therefore, was paramount from that point on, particularly as Shaw had been moved onto night work in the restaurant car of the Sheffield train, which meant overnight travel. Emily was left to fend for herself on certain nights of the week; something she was all too able to do.

But she was also adept at playing the dutiful wife, and at the start of September invited Bertram Shaw's mother to travel down from Northampton for a visit. Under the mistaken impression that Emily was her daughter-in-law, the invitation was accepted and the visit set up for Thursday, 12 September. The intention was probably to cement family relationships and maintain the charade that had been going on since the start of summer. Emily no doubt planned to stay away from her favourite haunts for a few days whilst Shaw's mother was there, not that it curbed her activities in the run-up to the visit. Using Bertram's absences to her advantage, Emily maintained a presence in the Rising Sun, intent on earning a few shillings whilst she still had the opportunity.

It was there, on Friday, 6 September, that she met, and changed forever, the life of Robert Wood. Working as an artist or designer for the London Stained Glass Works, Wood was an artist of some ability. He was a creative talent, designing posters, advertisements, comic characters and stained or painted glass. He was also a man who embraced whatever nightlife the capital could offer him, sharing that at times with a young woman, Ruby Young, whom he had known for around three years. It was an easy, at times perhaps intense, relationship. She had posed for him on numerous occasions, happy to be known amongst friends as an artist's model. The two had even been engaged for a few short weeks, but relations had cooled in the summer of 1907 as Wood was apparently not averse to sharing his favours, so to speak, with her friends. When he walked into the Rising Sun that Friday night, he therefore considered himself to be single and definitely available.

Their initial meeting was accidental: she wanted a penny for the gramophone. He provided it, and the two sat together and talked. At some point in the evening, a boy came into the pub selling cheap picture postcards, something Emily liked to collect. She had built up her collection over the years, and wanted to buy. But Wood told her he could create something much better, and either bought a postcard or took one from his pocket and then drew an image of a rising sun on the back. Impressed, Emily asked if he would send it to her. He agreed. But after giving her address, she told him to sign it with the name of Alice. Bertram would be jealous if he saw a man's name. The two then parted and Wood returned home.

On the following morning, Wood met her, again by accident, on Great College Street. She reminded him about the card, which he had not posted at that point, and she insisted he do so, stressing its importance for her collection. The meeting made an impression on Wood. There was nothing unattractive about Emily Dimmock, and Wood seems to have been smitten, presumably in full knowledge that she was a prostitute. Either way, he resolved to meet her again, though not that night. He stayed away from the pub that weekend, but did post the card off to her on Sunday evening, inviting her to meet him at 8.15 pm in the Rising Sun on the following night.

When the card arrived at St Paul's Road, Emily – or 'Phyllis' as Wood knew her – was in bed with seaman Robert Roberts. Whilst Wood had been dropping his postcard into the mail, Roberts and Emily had been sharing drinks and eventually sharing a bed. On leave from his ship, with several weeks' pay in his pocket, Roberts had bought his way into the apartment. The postcard with its invitation, which he read, clearly formed an obstacle to any future meeting. But Emily was not so easily swayed. When she met Wood that evening, as he had requested, it was still the sailor she took to her bed at the end of the night. Roberts actually stayed for the next two nights, always meeting Emily in the Rising Sun in the evening and apparently content enough to keep putting his hand in his pocket for as long as she was available. But on the Wednesday morning (11 September), as he prepared to leave, a letter arrived, signed 'Bertie', inviting her to the Eagle pub that night at 8.00 pm. Although Roberts watched as Emily read it through, he saw little of its content. Emily chose to burn it in the fire grate because, she told him, she did not want Bertram to know she had received it.

But Roberts obviously lived in hope. All too well aware of the planned meeting, he still expected that she would turn up at the Rising Sun, perhaps after 'Bertie' left, and there would be another night of pleasure if he coughed up the money, something he was more than willing to do. But she never showed up that night, and Roberts eventually returned to his own lodgings a disappointed man. The reason for the no-show was that Emily and Wood had met on Camden Road and walked to the Eagle, where they had stayed together, at times in conversation with bookseller Joseph Lambert, until around 11.00 pm. What happened after that has always remained a mystery.

What we do know is that next morning (Thursday, 12 September), Bertram Shaw arrived back at the apartment after his night in the restaurant car at around 11.30 am. What he found waiting for him was his mother, who had been unable to gain access as the door was still locked, his landlady unable to find a key to fit the lock. Both women believed Emily, who should have collected his mother from the railway station, had been delayed and inadvertently missed the Northampton train. But Bertram, perhaps suspicious and not prepared to wait, took the decision to break in. What he found justified the damage. Inside were clear signs of what he at first thought may have been robbery. The contents of a chest of drawers in the bedroom were spilled across the floor. The remains of a meal were on the table. Emily's postcard album was open on the chair by a window in the front room, the postcards loose, with some on the floor. The bed, seemingly unmade, had all the bedding piled up in a heap. Beneath that bedding, and covered by her own clothes, was the naked body of Emily Dimmock, her throat cut and clearly dead.

Detective Inspector Arthur Neil arrived on the scene at around three o'clock in the afternoon. His first impressions were that someone had searched the apartment looking for something after the murder. Drawers were open, their contents removed, and the window blinds partly raised, not for the purpose of robbery, but rather to allow light into the room. Neil quickly established that three gold rings had been left behind in one of the drawers, and not as an oversight, which suggested to him that robbery had not been the motive. The bed, he later reported, was saturated with blood, which had soaked through the mattress to the floor. The killer had obviously washed his hands after the killing, leaving bloody water in a basin. But Bertram Shaw did not completely agree with Neil's initial assessment. He claimed there had been a robbery. Missing, he later claimed, was a silver cigarette case and a silver curb chain with a vesta case attached, both of which had belonged to himself, and a purse containing money, a gold watch, gold wedding ring and gold curb ring that had belonged to Emily. However, this has always been contentious. Pawn shops were known to have been used by Emily, and many of these items may well have been used by her to raise money.

When Inspector Neil arrived at the apartment, Doctor John Thompson had been there since 1.00 pm and had already completed his initial examination of the body. In his opinion, the murder had taken place about seven or eight hours earlier, placing the time of death at around 5.00 am. The cut across Emily's throat had been made with some force, from left to right, with the windpipe completely severed. The doctor also noted a small cut on her right elbow, which he thought had been made by her attacker after death, possibly accidentally. He believed the attack had occurred whilst she had been asleep, the conclusion drawn from the position of Emily's body, which appeared, he reported later, to have been in a sleeping, comfortable position. He thought the killer had attacked her from behind, lifted her head to access the throat, cut the mattress accidentally in the process, and then pulled her left arm and hand behind her back after death.

This was a murderer, it seemed, who knew his business, but not one, the inspector believed, who would remain at large for too long. Emily, and how she earned her living, was known to police, which meant the obvious place to start their search was at the Rising Sun. Robert Roberts, who by this time had heard all about the discovery of her body, was sat inside the pub and wasted no time in waiting to be found. He surrendered himself to the first officers to enter the bar, well aware that he was likely to be classed as a suspect. In his initial interview with police, he made no secret of having known Emily, nor of the fact he had spent several nights sleeping with her. Crucially, however, he could prove his whereabouts the previous night, or at least provide enough witnesses to account for his movements. He could also offer some useful bits of background information on Emily, gleaned over the previous few days, all of which helped the investigation. But it was his account of the letter Emily had received on the morning of her death that grabbed their attention. It also led, eventually, to Robert Wood.

Inspector Neil sent officers back to the apartment on St Paul's Road on the Friday morning (13 September) to mount a second search and empty out the fire grate. Nothing new was found in the rooms, but they did find the burnt remains of the letter that Roberts told them was signed 'Bertie'. Piecing it together, and there was very little remaining, they were satisfied it was written to set up a meeting at the Eagle public house. Enquiries made there found barmaid Eilean Raven, who identified Emily, though not with absolute certainty, as the woman she had seen in the pub on the night of Emily's death. The letter retrieved from the fire grate was thus considered genuine, and Roberts' vague version of some of its contents accepted as fact, though its author remained a mystery.

Whilst all this was ongoing, Doctor Thompson revised his time of death. After examining the stomach contents, he had found the remains of Emily's last meal – meat, potatoes and stout – still largely intact. He decided that this finding, along with rigor mortis being present, shifted the time of death back to nearer 1.00 am. This time perhaps seemed more realistic to police, given that Emily had clearly eaten just before retiring that night and had eaten alone. But none of this did anything to identify the man she had supposedly met in the Eagle pub or the man they knew by this time she had been drinking with in the Rising Sun. All that changed on 25 September.

Bertram Shaw, who obviously knew of Emily's past, learned after her death of the various men she had been associating with whilst he was working on the night trains. Amongst the names mentioned was Robert Roberts. The two men met around 23 or 24 September, when Roberts told him there had been a third party, a man not found by police, a man who wrote a postcard with a drawing of a rising sun. Whether Roberts had ever told the police is debatable, but clearly at this stage of the murder investigation it had not been found. For Bertram, it perhaps seemed more relevant than the letter in the fire grate had to the police officers who carried out the original search of his apartment. His later search, which was obviously more thorough, found the card beneath lining paper in one of the drawers. On 25 September it was in the hands of Detective Inspector Neil, who in turn passed it on to the local press with a request they reproduce it in their newspapers and ask the public to identify the handwriting. They soon did.

So did Robert Wood's stepbrother. James Wood saw the published facsimile on the day it first appeared in the press. To his mind there was little doubt that Robert was its author, and when the two met later that same day he advised Robert to go to Scotland Yard. It was good advice, particularly as James had not been the first to point an accusing finger. The works foreman at the glass business employing Wood, Jack Tinkham, had already confronted him and forced an admission. But despite that and the obvious implications it had for him, Wood steadfastly refused to notify the police. Instead, he sought advice and alternatives from his eldest brother, Charles, and his wife, Bessie. Bizarrely, the three of them decided he ought to write a letter, not to the police, but to themselves; essentially a statement of fact in which Robert admitted to being the author of the postcard, but that he had no involvement in the murder, in the hope that after the inquest any evidence he could provide would be unnecessary. All three then signed it and posted it to the *poste restante* at St Martin's Le Grand, a part of the post office that held letters on behalf of clients.

It was a strange thing for Wood to have done, but by this time subterfuge had become familiar ground. Ruby Young, the artist's model he could have married, had been approached by him only days after the murder in an attempt to create an alibi should one ever be required, and she had readily agreed. She accepted his vague reasoning and promised, if ever questioned by police, to tell them she and Wood always met on a Monday and Wednesday. Bookseller Joseph Lambert had also had a call from Wood asking that he not discuss their meeting in the Eagle pub, citing the potential for scandal damaging to the Wood family name should it ever become known he had met the murdered woman in a public house. He was easily persuaded, probably because he never believed anyone would ever ask. So, up until the publication of the Rising Sun postcard, Wood had felt reasonably safe and out of reach of any police investigation. Admitting authorship and writing that letter to the *poste restante* obviously changed things. If his own family had recognized the handwriting and all that implied, so must Ruby, which meant the key alibi was in jeopardy. He was at her door within hours, desperate for her support. Realizing her confidence in him had been shaken, he admitted to his involvement with Emily Dimmock, but insisted he had not committed murder. What he needed was for her to tell police, if they ever found her, that they had been together on the night of the killing until after midnight. But Ruby was reluctant. What she had originally thought was a simple misdemeanour had become something far more complex, and afraid of the repercussions to herself, she initially refused. However, Wood's argument, that his innocence was assured, eventually proved too persuasive and forced a change of heart. For the next few days she held to her promise. Wood set up daily meetings to ensure she did not go back on her word, but the burden was too much and eventually she reneged, though not to the police. Instead she told a friend, who in turn told a newspaper reporter, and Inspector Neil arrested Robert Wood on 4 October as he met Ruby in Gray's Inn Road.

For the next four weeks police investigations intensified, but centred solely around Wood, with a number of identity parades being held, some more successful than others. Press speculation as to the murderer's identity prior to Wood's arrest had led to the publication of various descriptions, most erroneous, and the questioning of men known to use prostitutes in Camden. None, as far as I can see, were ever serious suspects. So the identity parades were key, not only in placing Wood in Emily Dimmock's company, but also to help track his movements. Today, we would no doubt treat them with a little more scepticism, but in 1907 there was probably little alternative, though in reality, once the postcard's author had been found, as far as the police were concerned the hunt was over. Police opinion hardened almost daily regarding Wood's guilt as they realized he could not account for his movements on the night of the killing and had lied to family, work colleagues and, of course, Ruby Young. However, suspicion and guilt are two different things.

Throughout October and November, Robert Wood made several appearances before magistrates at Clerkenwell Police Court. An attentive public followed the twists and turns through the press, all eager to know more about the 28-year-old artist, described in various newspapers as being clean shaven, 5ft 8in tall, with deep set eyes. But the actual trial is what pushed up newspaper circulation, not just in Camden but all around the country.

When it opened at the Old Bailey on 12 December before Mr Justice Grantham, it was to a packed courtroom. People from all walks of life, keen to gain access to the public gallery for what they believed would be the trial of the decade, had queued from early in the morning. Such was the interest in Robert Wood, the artist, that some of his work had been published by newspapers and magazines whilst he sat in Brixton prison, which allowed a far wider audience than was usual to see his talent displayed. There was also, no doubt, the draw of the country's most renowned and successful defence barrister, Sir Edward Marshall Hall, who was brought in by Wood's defence team once it had been agreed that his costs would be paid by Wood's employers. He was to prove an awesome adversary against the Crown, ably led by Sir Charles Mathews.

The police case essentially broke down into four parts: witness evidence that placed Wood on St Paul's Road in the early hours of the morning of Thursday, 12 September; proof that he had lied when he stated he had met Emily Dimmock on 6 September for the first time; the authorship of the letter, seen by Robert Roberts and destroyed in the fire grate inside Emily's apartment; and Wood's reason for trying to force Ruby Young to lie. Of evidence, or proof, that Wood had actually carried out the murder there was none. For Marshall Hall, that meant these were the areas that cast real doubt on the veracity of Robert Wood's denial. These, and only these, if believed by the jury, despite everything else being circumstantial, would put a noose around Wood's neck.

Marshall Hall began with coachman Robert McCowan, found by police and produced at the magistrates' hearings as the only witness to place Wood on St Paul's Road at what they believed was the key time. Reiterating his earlier evidence given at the magistrates' hearing, but with a little more precision, he told the court that on the morning of Emily Dimmock's murder, he had seen Wood leaving the murder house at precisely 4.48 am. Wood, he claimed, walked with a certain, identifiable swagger, and he saw him clearly in the glare of street lights coming down the steps in front of number 29. Of course, he was wrong, and Marshall Hall, who had clearly done his homework, knew that. The street lights on St Paul's Road had been switched off at 4.40 am., and as Marshall Hall pointed out, identifying Wood, or anyone else, in the gloom impossible. A hesitant McGowan had to agree, and under further questioning went on to admit that neither had the man he thought he saw come out of number 29. He had just assumed it was the murder house.

Showing that Wood had never met Emily Dimmock before 6 September, however, was far more difficult to prove. In the weeks leading up to the trial, there had been mounting evidence that the two of them had known each other since some point back in 1906. Various witnesses took the stand to tell the court that they had seen them together in the past, though these meetings were never noted as being serious or associated with any ongoing relationship. When examined further, conversations, drinks in a bar and meetings in the street were in most cases really all they were. The exception was Jack Crabtree, an ex-con, who had served several prison sentences. He had known Emily Dimmock for some time – at one point she even owed him money – so there can be no doubting a relationship of sorts had existed between them in the past. Crabtree also knew how she lived and earned money, and most of the men she met, which made his evidence cogent, even if a little unreliable. But it was his knowledge of Robert Wood's place in Emily's life that proved the most damaging. The two of them, he told the court, had been sleeping together back in 1906. He had seen them as a couple, and more importantly, Emily had asked him to pawn a silver cigarette case belonging to Wood and with his knowledge.

How true that was is impossible to know today, and was probably just as difficult to know over 100 years ago. Marshall Hall's intention, when questioning Crabtree, was not really to disprove his allegation, more to show his testimony as being unreliable: that it was the word of a man who had spent much of his life in a British prison; that he was a man not to be trusted, a man of dubious character. These arguments may have been effective on the jury, but there were too many others all prepared to say that Wood had lied in his police statement. I think it likely that perhaps they were right, and he and Emily had a past going back beyond the year in which she was murdered. Not that it really mattered. Whether or not he had known Emily – or 'Phyllis' as he tended to refer to her – did not prove he killed her.

Marshall Hall enjoyed more success, though mixed, over his questioning of Robert Roberts and the issue of the letter found in the fire grate. This was a fragmentary document and the court had put the remnants into the hands of various graphologists, most of whom were of the opinion that Wood had been the writer. However, very little text remained and Wood himself had essentially not really denied it either. But Marshall Hall, I think, perhaps had doubts and thought Wood's own vague acceptance of authorship a little questionable. The signature at the end of the letter – 'Bert' or 'Bertie' – remained contentious. According to Wood, he had signed the Rising Sun postcard 'Alice', at Emily's insistence, and never questioned it. This was done because she did not want Bertram Shaw, the man she lived with, to know she had received correspondence from other men. Surely, therefore, he would never have signed off the burned letter using a man's name, would he? It makes little sense today, and would, I guess, have made little sense back then. Certainly, under cross-examination, Robert Roberts was unable to confidently state the writing he saw in that letter had matched that of the Rising Sun postcard. However, he was adamant the name 'Bertie' had been used. For Marshall Hall, that was probably sufficient to cast doubt in the jury's mind that Wood had been the author of both.

But it was perhaps Marshall Hall's questioning of Ruby Young, and then Robert Wood himself, that swung the verdict in his favour. Ruby Young – already damaged by the murder, her character much besmirched, her standing in the community attacked and her belief in Wood shown to have been naïve at the very least – was treated with sympathy by the defence. To them, her very involvement created an opportunity. Wood, in that second attempt to reinforce his alibi through her, had clearly shown a lack of understanding concerning the timing of the murder and could not have been in any way involved. He wanted Ruby Young to tell police he had been with her only up to around midnight, which meant he had no idea Emily Dimmock had been murdered long after that time, rendering irrelevant any alibi she provided and, in effect, making her involvement unnecessary. That meant he could not have cut Emily's throat in the early hours of the morning, as Doctor Thompson claimed his autopsy had shown.

Clearly, the defence seemed satisfied that Wood had returned home on the night of the murder at around half past midnight, which his family had by this time all corroborated. He had believed he would be pulled into the police investigation if ever they discovered he had been involved with the victim on that night, which is why he sought the alibi from Ruby. What he had not realized is that the murder had taken place outside of the hours he had begged Ruby to perjure herself over, and this strongly suggested innocence.

When Robert Wood was put on the stand, Marshall Hall asked a very simple, straightforward question: 'Did you kill Emily Dimmock?' Wood gave an equally, simple but straightforward answer: 'How ridiculous, do you really want an answer?' 'Yes,' said his barrister. To which Wood replied: 'No.'

The response was emphatic, obviously expected, but with what had already transpired it clearly held the ring of truth for the jury. According to his testimony, he had taken Emily to the Eagle public house. He had created and posted the Rising Sun postcard. He had spoken to the bookseller, Joseph Lambert. But he had left her in the pub at eleven o'clock that night and returned home. His father had seen him before he retired to bed, as had his step-brother, James, and he had never been to the house at 29 St Paul's Road. The letter in the fire grate had not been written by him, but the remnant he had seen presented in court was probably a discarded paper from his notebook and possibly in his handwriting; something burnt as an addition to the letter but of no relevance to the court, something probably given to Emily whilst in the pub. Obviously there was more to his testimony, but essentially these facts were what mattered most, and the jury believed him.

A fifteen-minute consultation was all that was needed to return a 'not guilty' verdict, and six days after the start of the trial Robert Wood walked out of the Old Bailey a free man. Outside the courthouse he was welcomed by the thunderous applause of some 10,000 people. They had blocked off the traffic in Holborn, lined the roofs of nearby buildings and thronged nearby streets, such was the impact of the murder trial.

But did he kill Emily Dimmock? I would doubt it. Wood was really the only suspect for the police, and his dissimulation only strengthened their belief in his guilt. However, there are alternatives. In Patricia Cornwell's book *Ripper, The secret life of Walter Sickert*, she believes Sickert, the artist, may well have been involved. He lived in Camden at that time and painted *The Camden Town Murder* pictures, which were possibly inspired by Emily Dimmock's death. It is also no secret that Cornwell thought he could well have been Jack the Ripper, and the Dimmock murder does have similarities to the murder of Mary Kelly. There is also the fact that Emily was a prostitute who had suffered from syphilis and passed on the disease, reason enough perhaps for an unknown client bearing a grudge to pay a call, which may be why the case remains unsolved.

## Chapter 7

# The Summer House Shooting

*The murder of Caroline Mary Luard, 1908*

Charles Luard had been born into a military family, which meant he was almost predestined to follow his father into the Army. It was something that he apparently readily embraced, accepting a commission into the Royal Engineers aged 17. As a serving officer, he travelled to various parts of the British Empire, took part in the rearmament of the fortress at Gibraltar, supervised the reconstruction of the Household Cavalry barracks at Windsor, and in 1875 married Caroline Mary Hartley, whose mine-owning family owned Armathwaite Hall, near Cockermouth in what is now Cumbria. Eventual retirement from the Army with the honorary rank of major general brought the couple, along with their two sons, to Ightham Knoll, a country residence a mile or so outside Ightham village a few miles north-east of Sevenoaks. The property lay adjacent to the Frankfield estate in the heart of the Kent countryside, gave them access to a vast woodland acreage and was within easy reach of Godden golf club. Golf was a sport the major general had readily embraced in his retirement, as he had politics, serving for some fourteen years on the local council. He was supported in the main by his wife, who was particularly active on the social side of life and not without her own interests. Known locally to be a stalwart of numerous charities, Caroline ran the household staff and very much enjoyed her status within the local community. The couple led an essentially quiet life. The sons, as had been expected, had also joined the Army. The youngest, Eric, unfortunately died of fever whilst serving in Africa in 1903. But by the late summer of 1908 they had come to terms with that loss, celebrated 33 years of marriage and been accepted into the social and business world of Kent's moneyed class. Life seemed to be treating them well. Then, inexplicably, tragedy struck a second time and their fortunes were reversed.

On 24 August, at around 2.20 pm, Major General Luard and his wife decided to take a walk together. He wanted to go to the Godden clubhouse to collect his golf clubs, and she agreed to accompany him part of the way. As friends of Horace and Annie Wilkinson, owners of the nearby Frankfield estate, they had permission to use the footpaths traversing their woodland whenever they wished. Not wanting to use the road, they headed out toward Fish Pond Wood, some half a mile away from their home. Once there, they followed the path through the woods, past the Wilkinsons' summer house, La Casa, and on to a wicket gate a mile or so further on. At that gate they parted company. The major general walked down to the road and on to the golf club, while Caroline returned the way they had just come so that she could be back at Ightham Knoll to meet friends expected for tea. The time was around 3.00 pm.

At 3.15 pm, the Wilkinsons' gardener, Daniel Kettel, heard three shots fired in quick succession. Nearby, Anna Wickham, wife of the Wilkinsons' coachman, also heard the same shots. Both were about 400 yards away from the source of the gunfire; and both ignored it. After all, shots being fired in the countryside around the Frankfield estate was not uncommon, the shooting of game being a common occurrence. The major general, by this time well away from the vicinity of his afternoon's woodland walk, heard nothing. After collecting his golf clubs, he began his walk back home via the road at around four o'clock. This was later confirmed by the local vicar, who had stopped his car and offered to lighten his load and take the clubs from him. Charles accepted, but, in no apparent hurry, continued his walk, arriving back at Ightham Knoll around 4.30 pm. He was met at the house by Alice Stewart and her husband, Frank. They were new to the area and meant to take tea with his wife. Somewhat surprised, but not concerned, by Caroline's absence, he did the necessary. Then, after entertaining the couple for ten minutes or so, he made his apologies and offered to go in search of his wife whilst they waited. Alice thought that sensible, but, not wanting to be left behind, offered to accompany him. The pair left the house at about five o'clock. For Alice, perhaps the mind was willing but the body weak. She made her excuses after some fifteen minutes, citing forgotten guests of her own, and returned to the house. The major general was determined to continue. He followed the road, passed the Crown Point pub and then turned down Church Road, which eventually brought him back to the wicket gate where he and Caroline had parted company that afternoon. Once there, he paused before deciding to return by following the route of their afternoon walk from that wicket gate back to the Wilkinsons' summer house, and on toward Fish Pond Wood a second time and then home.

As he reached La Casa, which was hidden from view until the last minute by woodland and the curve of the bridle path, he clearly saw the body of his wife lying on the floor of the veranda. He realized the moment he approached her that she was dead; her face was covered in blood and she was cold to the touch. Her hat lay some feet away. Charles ran to the stables behind Horace Wilkinson's house, where he found the Wilkinsons' butler, Herbert Hardinge. He followed the major general back to the summer house to see for himself the nature of Caroline's wounds whilst others fetched the local constable, PC Marsh.

According to the local doctor, Mr Mansfield, who examined the body where it lay at around 7.40 pm, she had been shot in the head twice. One bullet had entered behind the right ear and had left powder burns; a second bullet had entered just below the left eye. He also believed it was possible she had been struck from behind before the shots were fired. The glove to her left hand had been removed and lay inside out on the ground. Three rings, confirmed later by Major General Luard, had been removed from her fingers. The pocket to her dress was ripped open and her purse was missing. The body was later carried to Ightham Knoll and placed in her bedroom.

Bloodhounds were on the scene the next morning in a bid to track the culprit, but proved unsuccessful, and Scotland Yard took over the investigation that same night. From the outset this was always going to be a difficult case, with an isolated location, no witnesses and, after twenty-four hours, no apparent motive. Robbery by vagrants or a passing tramp were offered up as the only real suggestion, though it is doubtful that the police ever gave real credence to the notion that some passing hop-picker with a gun had carried out the murder. The possibility was certainly considered, as this was an area of Kent familiar to itinerant labour seeking work and the hop-picking season had been poor in 1908. However, I believe from the outset that they never accepted the idea that the murder was anything other than a well-planned and executed killing. Yet evidence as to how or why was thin on the ground.

The first inquest opened at the Luards' home on 26 August, the roads around being clogged by traffic for much of the day as people travelled from all over the south of England to attend. Police were forced to restrict access even to the press, many of whom were barred from entering on the grounds that the house could not accommodate the numbers. Those who did gain entry were the envy of their peers left standing outside. Inside, they listened to the testimony from Major General Luard as he explained to Coroner Buss the events leading up to the discovery of his wife's body. They also heard from the witnesses to the sound of gunshots, both of whom felt that the first shot seemed a dull sound, as if the bullet fired hit something hard, and finally from Doctor Mansfield with his assessment of the murder scene. Little else happened that day because the venue was essentially too small, the coroner taking the decision to adjourn and reconvene at the nearby George and Dragon Hotel on 10 September.

Between the dates of the two inquests, Caroline Mary Luard's body was carried by horse-drawn hearse to Ightham Parish Church during heavy rain, followed by a cortege of ten carriages. There she was laid to rest beside her son, Eric, who had died in Africa five years earlier. The proceedings were watched by huge crowds, which, despite the appalling weather, had wanted to pay their last respects and stood in respectful silence beneath a canopy of umbrellas.

When the second inquest finally opened, again to huge public interest, it became clear no progress had been made in the police investigation. What had changed, however, was the view of how her death had occurred. Doctor Mansfield had already expressed an opinion that she had been struck down and then shot. In the time since he had made that statement, and the post-mortem, he had not changed his view, believing that damage to her straw hat along its back rim suggested a blow had been struck. But gun and rifle manufacturer Edwin Churchill, of Agar Street, The Strand in London, was of a differing opinion. After examining the body and the two bullets found inside the head of Caroline Luard, he told the court that death had not occurred how the doctor suggested. The first shot, he stated, had been fired from no more than an inch away from behind the right ear. That bullet, which had left powder burns, had not penetrated far into the skull because of hitting bone, hence the dull sound heard by the two witnesses living nearby. It was that shot, he insisted, that had knocked her to the ground. The second, killing shot had been fired from two or three inches away, whilst she was on the ground. The bullets were .320 revolver cartridges fired from a revolver that could have been purchased for about £1.

The court accepted this version of events. Police then explained the layout of the summer house, La Casa, the fact that the killer had not waited inside and how it had been locked up for over three months with no signs of entry being made during that time. The discovery of broken-down bracken and heather suggested a path away from the house into woodland as being the escape route followed by the killer. Unfortunately, heavy rain following the murder had destroyed any other useful evidence. The stolen rings had also not been recovered. The police also explained that they had taken three guns from Major General Luard's house for examination, none of which could have fired the fatal shot.

The inquest closed without resolution, and from that point on nothing else was ever found to explain away the murder of Caroline Luard. However, the tragedy did not end there. Charles Luard's second son, who had been notified of his mother's death, was travelling back to England from where he had been stationed in South Africa. Whilst he waited for his son's return, the major general decided he could no longer remain living at Ightham Knoll and made the decision to put the lease up for sale. On 17 September, after much of the house's contents had been packed away, he was invited to stay with a good friend, Colonel Charles Warde. He accepted, but during that evening something happened to Charles Luard. In the early hours of 18 September, having retired to bed in apparent good spirits, he wrote a letter to the colonel:

'My Dear Warde,

I am sorry to have to return your kindness and hospitality and long friendship in this way, but I am satisfied it is best to join her in the second life at once, as I can be of no further use to anyone in the future in this world, of which I am tired, and in which I do not wish to live any longer.

I thought that my strength was sufficient to bear up against the horrible imputations and terrible letters which I have received since that awful crime was committed, which has robbed me of my happiness. And so it was for long and the kindness and sympathy of so many friends kept me going. But somehow, in the last day or two, something seems to have snapped, the strength has left me, and I care for nothing except to join her.

So good-bye, dear friend.

Yours affectionately

C E Luard'

Major General Charles Edward Luard died as he stepped in front of a train that morning. The same day, his son finally arrived back at Ightham Knoll from South Africa to discover the second tragedy for his family. Charles Luard had felt driven to take his own life, it is believed, because of the number of accusing letters he received after his wife's death.

His suicide essentially brought the case to an unsatisfactory close. The murder was never solved and new evidence was never produced, although there was one arrest. In a botched attempt to solve the case, police arrested David Talbot Woodroof. Educated at Little Thurlow, Suffolk, Woodroof spoke six languages, had been married once, was about 60 years old and at that stage of his life was in straitened circumstances. Arrested in Maidstone, he appeared before Sevenoaks magistrates on 20 September, charged with the murder of Caroline Luard. Superintendent Taylor, of Kent constabulary, told the court he had been arrested whilst already in custody for common assault. Woodroof pleaded not guilty and was ably defended by solicitor Mr House, who insisted his client had been arrested simply because at some time in the past he had owned a revolver. The court, quite sensibly, asked to see evidence or proof corroborating the police belief that he was the real murderer. Police could offer none, the case was thrown out and Woodroof returned to obscurity.

Since that date there has been no further progress, but there has been speculation. Some years ago it was suggested that the Luard murder had been carried out by John Dickman, a man executed in 1910 for the railway murder of a man named Nesbit. The conviction has always been contentious, and Sir Sydney Orme Rowan Hamilton, one-time Chief Justice of Bermuda, who published an account of the Dickman case, believed Dickman may not have killed Nesbit but that he had killed Caroline Luard. Hamilton claimed the murder came about after Dickman had advertised in *The Times* for financial help and Caroline Luard had sent him a cheque, the value of which remains unknown. Dickman had then committed fraud by amending this cheque's value, and she had discovered it. After writing to him, a meeting had been arranged – without Major General Luard's knowledge – at La Casa, where Dickman shot her dead. Hamilton believed that a conspiracy against Dickman at his trial for the Nesbit killing by friends of the dead Major General Luard ensured his conviction for a murder he may not have committed becaue of a murder they were certain he had. This sounds implausible to me, but Dickman did have a chequered past so can never be totally ruled out.

For many people, the killer has always been Caroline Luard's husband. Their marriage was perhaps not as secure as history would have us believe. This certainly has to be a possibility, despite the tragedy of his suicide. Nevertheless, it is difficult to show he had the opportunity when the timings given in court of his movements that day, as reported by witnesses who saw him, placed him well away from the murder scene when the shots are known to have been fired. Two independent witnesses to the sound of gunfire cannot be ignored.

I do not believe he carried out the shooting. But I have a suspicion that the killer was known to Caroline Luard, and quite possibly she had arranged a meeting at the summer house. Everything about the shooting suggests to me it was a deliberate and calculated act. This was no robbery gone wrong; the attacker intended only one thing: murder.

*Chapter 8*

# The Kidwelly Poisoning

*The murder of Mabel Greenwood, 1919*

In 1896, Harold Greenwood, whilst studying law, met and married Mabel, the younger daughter of the Bowater paper-making family. They were one of London's most successful businesses at that time, supplying newsprint to the likes of the *Daily Mail* and the *Daily Chronicle*. The family lived at Bury Hall in Edmonton, north London, a 300-year-old Jacobean house that was once a notable landmark but has since been demolished. Whether Harold had ever been impressed by it is not known. The couple certainly did not hang around for long after their marriage. By 1898 he had bought himself into a partnership as a newly qualified solicitor with the Llanelli-based firm of Johnson & Stead, and the couple moved to Kidwelly, some 12 miles from Carmarthen in South Wales. Within a few years that partnership had been dissolved, and he began operating on his own account. Based in Llanelli, with an office on Frederick Street, Harold's business mainly consisted of legal work around house purchasing and general property ownership, with a few clients operating in the financial sector. Though not hugely successful, he earned enough from the business to enable he and Mabel to move from Broomhill, their first house, to The Priory, and by November 1916 to buy the very impressive Rumsey House. By this time they were a family of six, along with three servants, an outside gardener and Mabel's sister, Edith Bowater, who paid a weekly rent and part-owned some of the house's furnishings. To neighbours, they appeared to be an average, comfortable, middle-class family with a reasonably solid marriage.

But Mabel Greenwood's health had been failing since the birth of their last child in 1909. Suffering from a weak heart, occasional fainting fits and various other undefined disabilities, she was under the care of Kidwelly doctor Thomas Griffiths. Although none of these ailments ever appeared to interfere with or stop her running an effective household, what they had done was affect the quality of her life and create in her mind a fear of cancer – an understandable fear perhaps, in light of her constant battle with ill-health, but one she managed effectively.

By the start of 1919, however, there had been a change. Mabel began to complain of pains in or around her heart. She had been unable to sleep on her left side for almost a year, complaining that to do so created a sense of suffocation. The doctor could find nothing to indicate any deterioration in the heart valves, and Harold suggested they write to her brother in London and ask that he bring a heart specialist to Wales. She agreed, but after the letter had been written, refused to allow it to be posted. Frustrated, Harold suggested she undergo a complete medical check. She had planned a holiday to Portishead in June, and he thought after her return would be a good time. She again agreed. Nothing more was said, leastways not by Mabel, but it appears that Harold found it difficult to keep his own counsel. Rumour then spread that Mabel was seriously ill, and that she could, and probably would, die as a result. It generated a great deal of sympathy amongst their neighbours and increased the number of visitors to the house, all trying to ascertain for themselves just how ill she really was. But, it would seem, such rumours never brought another doctor to their door. Life went on, and Mabel did her best to promote an image of her own well-being. On 8 June, she attended church alone. The following day, she had tea with a neighbour. A week later, she was fitted for a new dress to take on her holiday, and on Saturday, 14 June, she called on Martha Morris. Martha was a woman Mabel knew well, having acted as nurse to her daughter, Irene, and still worked at Rumsey House. She was also a woman Mabel obviously felt she could talk to. Martha would later recall that when they met, Mabel appeared to be very ill. Mabel told her she had been suffering from diarrhoea, felt her heart was failing and had been depressed. Nevertheless, that Saturday was a busy day. After leaving Martha, she bought some Burgundy wine and she and Harold ate an early lunch. She had promised to attend a tennis meeting at Ferryside, some 5 miles away, and was keen to go, despite feeling unwell. Harold walked with her to Kidwelly railway station, where he left her in the company of Kidwelly's vicar, David Jones. The pair of them made the journey together, and she returned home later that evening.

Mabel and Harold were supposed to have attended church on Sunday morning, but she complained of feeling too ill and stayed at home. He decided to work outside on his car, which he did until lunchtime. They had a roast joint, the usual vegetables, followed by gooseberry tart and custard, washed down by burgundy wine for her and whisky for him.

By mid-afternoon, Mabel was again complaining of diarrhoea but was not particularly debilitated by it. The rest of the afternoon was spent in or around the garden, but at around 6.30 pm she began to vomit. Harold fetched Doctor Griffiths, who instructed the family to put her to bed and feed her sips of brandy and soda water. He then returned to his surgery and sent over a bottle of medicine containing bismuth. At around eight o'clock her condition had deteriorated, and Nurse Jones, a local district nurse known by the family, was sent for. She stayed for an hour, during which Mabel complained of a sore throat when she swallowed. The nurse returned at ten o'clock, followed by Doctor Griffiths half an hour later. By this time her condition had worsened, but the doctor remained convinced it was no more than a severe case of gastritis or something similar and left to return to his surgery. The burden of care thus fell on the shoulders of Nurse Jones, who treated Mabel with brandy, milk and soda water, all taken separately and in small doses every fifteen minutes or so. But the diarrhoea was unrelenting and at around midnight, concerned that Mabel's condition had deteriorated significantly, she sent Harold Greenwood out to fetch the doctor back. According to her later testimony, the doctor visited for the last time at 1.00 am. This would later become a point of contention, Dr Griffiths arguing he had no recollection of that early morning visit. Whatever the truth as to the time, he did prescribe two pills, which Harold Greenwood fetched from his surgery in the early hours that morning. The nurse administered both, as the doctor's written instructions had indicated, but Mabel fell into a coma. She never regained consciousness and died at 3.30 am on 16 June.

Within a few hours of the death, Harold Greenwood was in his car and on his way to Llanelli. Once there he met with Llewllyn Jones, part-owner of the *Llanelli Mercury* and a man he had known for twenty years, their association going back to the time of Greenwood's arrival in Wales. At that time he had helped the newspaper financially, and in return, Jones had helped bring new clients to his infant solicitor's practice. Firm friends, the two men had met on an almost daily basis, with Greenwood readily accepted into the Jones family circle, though as far as I can tell never at Rumsey House. Therefore, in many ways it was in no way unusual that he should have made the journey into Llanelli to share his grief with his old friend. There was also the added attraction of Llewellyn's daughter, Gladys, a woman who was to figure prominently in his life in the months that followed. But on that day her role was simply to accompany him to town to help him buy mourning clothes. Whilst this occupied much of Greenwood's day, back at Rumsey House there were other, more pressing matters. Nurse Jones had privately expressed concerns over Mabel's death. At that point she could have requested Doctor Griffiths to re-examine the cause of death and perhaps call for a post-mortem examination. She chose not to, which is perhaps understandable given the doctor's status in relation to her own. But those doubts, directly or indirectly, caused a stir amongst the Kidwelly community. The good doctor, who may even have had his own doubts, though perhaps for different reasons, as would surface later, certainly never expressed them and was quick to cite cause of death as heart failure probably caused by a faulty heart valve. The diagnosis was an expected fit with the illness he had been treating over the years and a reasonable conclusion to have reached; or at least so he believed. The Greenwood family never challenged it, and on Thursday, 19 June Mabel Greenwood was buried in St Mary's churchyard.

That ought to have put an end to any speculation about the cause of her death, and probably would have had it not been for Harold Greenwood's apparent naivety. Awareness of the gossip around his purported involvement in it seemed not to cause him any anxiety. Nor did he appear, outwardly at least, to be the grieving husband for any reasonable length of time. Within a few weeks, rumour of his romantic involvement, first with Florence Phillips, who had been a long-time friend of the Greenwood family, then with Doctor Griffiths' sister, Mary, had begun to spread. By September these names had been replaced with that of Gladys Jones, the woman who had helped him buy his mourning clothes and a woman he often lunched with at the *Mercury* offices. The latter relationship was especially frowned on because she was known to be engaged to soldier Frank Russell, and had been since 1915. Duplicity of this sort was disapproved of by both community and church. But, of course, they were wrong; at least on one count, as the engagement had been ended by Gladys in a letter written that month. In turn, that meant their disapproval was misplaced, but the gossip was right. Whether it was also the cause of Harold Greenwood announcing to the world that he was to marry her in October is debateable. But once his wife had died, he had obviously become an eligible bachelor. There is an argument that would suggest that, while he did not have a hand in his wife's death, he did remarry in a hurry simply because he did not enjoy his single status; that perhaps it was difficult to work and live with his family at Rumsey House without another woman in his life. Marrying Gladys, a woman he had known since she had been a child, was an obvious choice. There is also the fact that since Mabel's death, he had lost access to her private income, which had been set up by her father and died with her.

Rumsey House was a large property to maintain and run. The salary of a local solicitor was perhaps not sufficient to sustain the lifestyle he, and his family, had grown used to. Either way, news of the impending marriage swept like wildfire around Kidwelly, swelling local belief that he had committed murder to facilitate it.

This time the rumour and speculation seemed to have foundation. Marrying so soon after the death was perceived as either guileless or ingenuous. The people of Kidwelly tended to believe the former. Harold Greenwood, of course, believed neither. He had made it clear to his family weeks earlier that he would countenance no objection and had poured scorn on the doubters, threatening libel action against those who refused to believe there had been no past transgression involving Mabel's death. It has to be doubtful, however, that he would ever have attempted legal action, it being far too costly and possibly far too damaging. Either way, it was not about to stop the marriage, which went ahead without hitch on 1 October 1919. It was a mistake, as there is no doubt that this marriage, just three months after the death of his wife, was the catalyst that triggered the investigation police later felt compelled to launch. Superintendent Jones and Inspector Nicholas of the Llanelli force finally knocked at their door three weeks later. The meeting, cordial and probably not totally unexpected, was intended to explore the events surrounding Mabel's death that June night, and would eventually prove contentious. Greenwood subsequently refused to sign what essentially police claimed was a statement, citing as his reason various inaccuracies in the text. The police, on the other hand, claimed it to be an unsolicited statement of fact that was admissible as valid evidence in support of their investigations. Whatever the truth, it was clearly the first link in a chain of enquiry that was going to stretch across the winter months of late 1919 and early 1920. In a painstakingly slow, and at times extremely arduous investigation, Llanelli police officers pulled together their accumulated results into a lengthy report, which they presented to the Chief Constable of Carmarthenshire, Picton Philipps, in March 1920. Satisfied as to the veracity of the evidence that had been gathered, he then presented it to the Home Office. On 16 April 1920, Coroner Nicholas, having been informed of the details uncovered by police and after some consultation with other interested parties, accepted the contention that there could be a case to answer and ordered an exhumation. A post-mortem followed that same morning at Kidwelly Town Hall, conducted by Doctor Alexander Dick, in the presence of three other doctors, one of whom was Kidwelly's Doctor Griffiths.

The results of the post-mortem examination showed that Mabel Greenwood had not suffered from heart failure due to heart valve problems, but that all her organs contained traces of arsenic. The amount was eventually confirmed by the Home Office's own expert, Doctor Willcox, as being 18 milligrams, or around a quarter of a grain. That meant, taking into account her vomiting and diarrhoea, that she had probably swallowed around two grains, maybe slightly more, which was enough to cause her death. An inquest, opened and adjourned on the day of the post-mortem, resumed on 15 June at Kidwelly Town Hall. After a long hearing, the jury unanimously found that Mabel had been murdered by arsenic, the poison that killed her having been administered by Harold Greenwood.

The verdict's announcement was almost drowned out by people applauding the jury's decision. Greenwood was never likely to find much sympathy amongst the people of Kidwelly.

Plain clothes police officers then travelled to Rumsey House, where Greenwood was arrested. Scotland Yard's Detective Inspector Haig interviewed him in the cells at Kidwelly police station, outlining the charge against him. He was then bustled out of the police station through a huge, hostile crowd that had been gathering since the verdict had been announced, and driven to Llanelli. The following morning, he made his first, brief appearance in the magistrates' court and was remanded in custody for a week. He reappeared on 25 June, but had to wait until 1 July for the full hearing to begin. This lasted three days, at the end of which he was committed to stand trial at the Carmarthen Assizes.

For the next four-and-a-half months, Greenwood languished in jail whilst the prosecution put together their case and his defence, led by the indomitable Sir Edward Marshall Hall KC, planned its demolition. In truth, the Crown's case was weak. Investigations by police had failed to discover arsenic in their searches of Rumsey House, its outbuildings or its stables. Nor had they been able to show that Greenwood had, at any time, purchased poison, the exception being weedkiller, which he had bought quite openly and never concealed. Even his association with Gladys Jones, which had resulted in the rush to wed and had been thought by police to have been instrumental in his planning of Mabel's death, proved false. No witness could be found to show the pair had been involved in any long-standing affair before the murder. Neither was evidence forthcoming of any other affair throughout his twenty years of living in Kidwelly. Harold Greenwood, it would appear, had been faithful to his wife. The only contentious piece of evidence discovered was that he had bought a ring on 12 July 1919 for £55 and given it to Gladys. It was a ring, he explained, intended for his daughter, but he had changed his mind and given it to Gladys after deciding he wanted to marry her. This was a perfectly reasonable and rational decision, though to the investigating officers a little too close to his wife's death and, perhaps, an indication that all had not been well within the marriage.

When the trial opened on 2 November 1920 before Mr Justice Shearman, the prosecuting counsel, led by Sir Edward Marlay Samson KC, addressed the jury for two hours. Much of that opening speech centred around two distinct facts. One, that arsenic had been the cause of death; and two, that it had been administered by Harold Greenwood using Eureka weedkiller, which he had purchased on two occasions in February and April 1919. The 60 per cent arsenic content of the weedkiller was easily dissolvable in both water or red wine. Essentially, Marlay Samson was instructing the jury that from the outset it would be the medical evidence that mattered. There could be no doubt, he argued, that Mabel Greenwood had swallowed poison. The question for them was whether she did it herself or it was administered by the man in the dock.

The facts appeared irrefutable, but Marshall Hall, who had no intention of challenging the findings of the autopsy, had every intention of challenging the amount of arsenic discovered. The finding of a quarter of a grain, he argued, was insufficient to have caused death, and he was right. But he also knew the quarter grain found was residual, vomiting and diarrhoea being responsible for removing the greater amount. Whilst it was never going to be a winning argument, it was put before the jury to create doubt and uncertainty. I believe that for Marshall Hall, the case revolved around local doctor Thomas Griffiths, whom he believed could have been guilty of a serious error. Marshall Hall had realized at the start of the trial that in both the inquest and the magistrates hearing, the doctor had told the court that on the night of Mabel Greenwood's death he had sent over to Nurse Jones two pills at around 1.00 am, though the time had been disputed. These pills, he had stated, were morphia pills, each pill containing half a grain of morphia. Neither hearing had challenged those statements. But the defence team recognized that if this evidence were true, then Mabel Greenwood would have died of morphia poisoning. The dosage was lethal. The doctor had also sent over a bottle containing bismuth, intended to settle the stomach. But in his surgery had been found a bottle of Fowler's mixture, which looked the same, and Fowler's mixture contained arsenic. If the doctor had made a mistake with the pills, could he not also have done the same over the bismuth mixture? This theme was to run throughout the trial, constantly sowing the seeds of doubt, but this was not the only aspect of the case that Marshall Hall had to dismantle.

From the outset, it was clear that the trial would really fall into three distinct acts. The first was to set the scene, describing and showing that Mabel Greenwood had suffered ill-health for some considerable time and how Doctor Griffiths had been a regular visitor to Rumsey House. This aspect was easy to achieve, as various witnesses were brought to court and testified as to her well-being or lack of it. However, to add credence to the Crown's belief that the poison had been administered by the defendant, they had to show the jury how that could have been achieved. The second act, and by far the more contentious, was to prove Mabel had died as a result of swallowing arsenic and just how it had been administered. The prosecution centred on the Sunday lunch, the only time that day, they argued, where the opportunity had presented itself to poison her. However, it could not have been in the food, as all at the table that day ate the same meal. It therefore had to have been in the wine, the drink no other diner than Mabel had taken. The bottle had been placed on the table by housemaid Hannah Williams, according to whose testimony it was not burgundy, as had been believed, but port wine: in a black bottle with a red label.

Hannah was asked: 'And are you quite certain that the bottle on the table on this Sunday was a black bottle with a red label with black letters and the word "Port" on it?' She replied: 'It had "Port Wine" written on it.'

Burgundy may have been Mabel's usual tipple, but not on that particular Sunday. Furthermore, on the Monday morning that same bottle had disappeared from the sideboard where it had stood twenty-four hours earlier. Challenged on her version of events, Hannah remained adamant, adding that prior to the meal Harold Greenwood had also been in the china cupboard, where there was a sink, which raised the possibility he had doctored the wine before lunch had been served. Just how reliable was her evidence is debatable, Hannah not being a wine drinker, and under questioning she was proven at times to be vague concerning events that Sunday afternoon.

Nevertheless, when taken at face value, this in itself was damaging to Harold Greenwood. As Sunday lunch was an obviously regular weekly event, he would have known his wife's habits. Her custom of being the sole wine drinker at the table created the means. Being in that china cupboard out of sight of everyone else was the opportunity. There is no doubting the impact this had on the jury, but it was the third and final act in that courtroom, the medical evidence, that would decide Harold Greenwood's fate.

This testimony was key to understanding whether or not the belief that poison had been administered was valid, and there was a huge amount of it. Various doctors had been brought to Carmarthen, all experts of one sort or another. Their task was to either reinforce the prosecution's case or refute it. Many hours were spent hearing testimony from those that had carried out or witnessed the post-mortem, the results being questioned and their meaning analyzed, and many more hours on trying to understand the limited scientific evidence. Theories were examined concerning just how arsenic manifested itself once digested, the quantities needed to kill and the amount that already existed within the human body. Despite the compelling nature of all this evidence, none of which could really be disputed to any profound degree, only the disclosure of the treatments prescribed by Doctor Thomas Griffiths, Kidwelly's local GP, made any real impact.

By the end of the trial, Marshall Hall had sown enough doubt around the conclusions of the medical men to change the jury's thinking. If arsenic had killed Mabel Greenwood, how had it been administered, and had Harold Greenwood been shown, and proven, to have fed it to his wife? Or could there have been another cause? Had a doctor, in error, supplied the lethal dose and then administered the killing blow with two small brown tablets? In his final summation to the jury, Marshall Hall outlined his thinking:

'I contend that I am justified in suggesting that Dr Griffiths made an unfortunate mistake that was colossal in its results. It is admitted that the bismuth mixture would not cause discomfort to the patient. It is admitted that arsenic solution would cause some irritation. It is proved in this case that, when Mrs Greenwood took the medicine, she complained that it caught her throat … I am not making any allegation against Dr Griffiths. I am submitting that this was a mistake on his part … Then we come to the one o'clock visit, about which there is a mystery. Why did Dr Griffiths, who remembered everything else so well, not remember that visit? I would suggest to you why. Because he knew at one o'clock some sort of suspicion may have crossed his mind that she had accidentally taken a dose of arsenic or some other kind of poison sent by him in mistake.'

He went on to explain to the jury that he believed the doctor had compounded this mistake by sending the nurse two morphia tablets, and had not been explicit enough in his instructions as to how they were to be given. She administered both of them, and Mabel Greenwood died.

For the jury, this explanation and the fact that no real evidence had been produced by the Crown to show Harold Greenwood had committed murder was probably enough to return a 'not guilty' verdict. It was a decision supported by the press, who in their editorials later that day believed the decision to have been valid based on what had been produced in court. For Harold Greenwood, the stigma of this trial, and whether guilty or not, had a profound effect on the rest of his life. He died in Hertfordshire on 17 January 1929, where he had lived under the name of Pilkington.

But did Greenwood poison his wife? I would doubt it. I think Sir Edward Marshall Hall was on firm ground when he took on the case. There was not, and still is not, any viable evidence that would show the solicitor had murdered his wife. Did the doctor, inadvertently, cause her death? That is obviously impossible to know. But enough seeds of doubt were sown to cause indecision amongst the jurors, which was Marshall Hall's job. It certainly seems strange that the symptoms exhibited by Mabel Greenwood, which clearly were of arsenical poisoning – the burning throat, vomiting and diarrhoea – did not seem to have occurred until the evening of 15 June. If she had consumed the poison during the Sunday lunch, surely her symptoms would have manifested much earlier. In conclusion, whoever administered it could only have been the doctor, the nurse, Harold Greenwood or his daughter, Irene. They were the only people around that bedside throughout the whole of the times that mattered. One of them possibly got away with murder.

*Chapter 9*

# The Railway Murder

*The murder of Florence Nightingale Shore, 1920*

O n the afternoon of 12 January 1920, Florence Nightingale Shore and her good friend Mabel Rogers made their way across London to Victoria station. For Florence, who had been staying in London since arriving back from France in November of the previous year, it was the continuation of a much-needed holiday and a respite from the horrors of trench warfare in France and Belgium. Europe had been her home since the outbreak of war back in 1914, when she initially joined the French Red Cross, where her experience of battle injuries gained in the Boer War had proven invaluable in caring for soldiers of the French Tenth Army. Much of her time had been spent in the various front-line clearing stations and field hospitals tending to French African troops: Zouaves, Turcos and Senegalese. In 1915, a year after arriving in France, she had joined Queen Alexandra's Imperial Nurses and, as the war progressed, worked in various front-line hospitals and travelled with the wounded on hospital trains, including those at the end of the war carrying German wounded back to Cologne. Demobbed in time for Christmas, she was spending quality time with Mabel, a woman she had known for twenty-six years, and was intending to travel south to visit friends at St Leonards on the 3.20 pm train.

The pair arrived at the station with time to spare, and Florence boarded her train at around quarter past three. Essentially a train of two halves, the London to Hastings train consisted of eleven carriages, and travelled direct as far as Lewes, where the front half was uncoupled and went on to Eastbourne; the rear carriages to Hastings. Florence walked virtually the whole length of the train and entered the last but one carriage, third-class non-smoking. No other passengers boarded at that stage, so Florence initially had the compartment to herself. Mabel helped carry in her luggage – a suitcase, a small portmanteau and a black silk handbag – then sat beside her for two or three minutes. The conversation was necessarily brief, cut short by the sound of the guard's whistle and the slamming of carriage doors. Goodbyes said, Mabel then hurriedly stepped down from the carriage to wave Florence off from the platform, at which point a young man, dressed in a brown suit, pushed past her and climbed into the same compartment as the train departed.

It arrived into Lewes station on time, but a train pulling eleven carriages meant that not every carriage could reach the platform. Station master Mr Marchant, as had become common practice, sent a guard, Henry Duck, down the platform slope toward the rear two carriages to assist anyone needing help to leave the train. On this occasion no-one did, but the guard reported later that there had been one man – young, around 25 years old, wearing an overcoat and white muffler – who had jumped down on his own and wandered off into the station. At the time it aroused no suspicion, and, after being uncoupled, the rear carriages became the Hastings train, scheduled to make several stops en route. At Polegate, three platelayers – George Clout, Thomas Ransom and Ernest Thomas – climbed into the carriage where Florence sat, her head resting on the back of the seat, slumped as if sleeping, with her feet on top of a newspaper on the floor of the carriage and an open book on her lap. By this time it was dark outside, and the poorly lit carriage meant that for the fifteen-minute journey to Bexhill they believed she was sleeping and so paid scant attention, though they had noticed what looked like dried blood on her face. It was only when the train pulled into Bexhill station that the significance of that blood became apparent and they called the station guard.

Florence was found to have been severely beaten around the head. Police later hypothesized that her body had been purposely moved away from the window on the platform side, where she would probably have been seen more clearly by the platelayers, to give the appearance of sleep. Her coat collar had been lifted in the process to frame her face, adding to the illusion of a woman resting after a long journey. Subterfuge at its best, it had worked long enough for her killer to escape, essentially unnoticed. Taken to East Sussex Hospital in Hastings, Florence died with friend Mabel beside her four days later on 16 January, having never regained consciousness.

For the public at large, the very mention of the name Nightingale, synonymous with nursing, the Crimean War and the Victorian age, meant a heightened interest in the case. Newspapers from all around the country were keen to follow the police investigation, each ensuring close scrutiny of the growing manhunt as it expanded across southern England. All were appalled at the callous, brutal slaying of a woman who had given her entire life to the care of others, and a goddaughter of the woman responsible for the restructuring of the entire nursing profession. Her godmother, Florence Nightingale, had, by her own sheer determination, forced through best medical practices as a fundamental principle of care in the treatment of soldiers, achieved a status for the nursing profession never before recognised. It was a status the 53-year-old on that Hastings train had upheld and a name she had carried with great credit, though probably with a measure of anonymity.

During the war years she had been known amongst the French African soldiers as the 'white queen', the name Nightingale carrying little weight in that setting and even less meaning. I would also guess that a degree of anonymity surrounded much of her career, which had started in the Royal Infirmary, Edinburgh, in 1893, and for many of the sixteen years she had spent as a midwife. But her name had been proudly displayed on her Boer War campaign medal, and again on the prestigious Royal Red Cross Medal awarded for her unstinting bravery and sterling work with the war wounded.

She was the daughter of Offley Bohun Shore, whose family had risen to prominence during the English Civil War, when they had supported Charles I from their base in Derbyshire. The family had at one time owned the Shore Bank in Sheffield and built Tapton Hall. Their fortunes took a severe downturn when the bank eventually failed, closing in 1843, the family forced to sever their Sheffield connections and move south. Cousin William Shore eventually inherited the Lea Hurst estate in Derbyshire from Peter Nightingale and as a result assumed the Nightingale name, becoming father to Florence (forever known to history as 'the lady with the lamp'). Florence's cousin, Florence Nightingale Shore, became her goddaughter in 1867

With a background that was clearly upper-class, it must have seemed odd to the investigating police that she had travelled third-class when she could have afforded better. It must also have caused a degree of consternation that she had been targeted in this way. Florence made no outward show of wealth and she carried little money. According to her friend, Mabel, when she boarded the train at Victoria station she only had three £1 notes on her, a train ticket and a small amount of jewellery. The jewellery consisted of a single ring with five inset diamonds, a gold necklace chain with two amethyst drops, a gold wristlet watch and a gold ring set with turquoise, valued at around £100 (£3,000 today). All were missing when she was found in the carriage. The question thus arose as to whether or not robbery had been the motive, or whether there was more to her death than at first believed.

At her inquest, Doctor Bernard Spilsbury, the Home Office pathologist whose forensic evidence had previously helped convict Hawley Harvey Crippen, poisoner Frederick Seddon and the 'Brides in the bath killer', George Smith, told the court that she had been struck on the head at least three times with something heavy, possibly the butt of a revolver. He concluded that there were no signs of a struggle and the blows had been struck whilst she had been seated. As a result, there was no doubting the murder was a deliberate and intentional act. The police were reasonably certain the attack had been carried out between Victoria station and the first stopover at Lewes, probably as the train passed through Merstham tunnel, the first half hour or so of the train journey being overlooked by housing lining both sides of the track and it still being daylight. They were also convinced that the man seen leaving the train by Henry Duck, the railway guard, had been the killer and a man familiar with the southern railway network, or at least the Brighton line. He was at least familiar enough to know that once he had left that train he had three options if he was to remain anonymous. One was to walk much of the length of the standing train, re-board nearer the front and travel on to Eastbourne. Another was to mingle in with the crowds disembarking, some thirty to fifty people, and cross over to another platform. The final option was to stay on the platform and board either the train to Seaford or that to Tunbridge Wells. Any one of these choices meant no crossing of the ticket barrier. The police thus believed that he had travelled to Lewes before, and was familiar with the station's layout and the onward travel available. There were no other clues.

On Monday, 19 January her coffin was laid at the entrance to the chancel of Christ Church, St Leonards, and at 7.45 am the next day Requiem Mass was celebrated. Florence's body was then taken by car to St Saviour's Church, Ealing, for the funeral. The coffin was draped in the Union flag and carried through huge crowds that had lined the streets around the church to pay their own respects to a war hero. Mounted police and officers on foot then cleared a passage for the funeral cortege as the coffin made its slow progress to the City of Westminster cemetery at Hanwell, where she was buried.

Over the next few months, police enquiries continued but nothing was ever found. The stolen jewellery never surfaced. It came to light, toward the end of the year, that Scotland Yard had harboured a belief that Florence could have been murdered by a known killer, Percy Topliss. He fitted the profile, was a so-called master of disguise, had the right build, fitted the age profile and was serving in the Army. He was also known to have been absent without leave at the time of Florence's murder, and was a known killer. Furthermore, police knew that during the war he had served in the Army Medical Corps, though not in France. Their suspicion was thus not without foundation, though the link had to have been tenuous. The murder of Florence was unlike anything Topliss had been involved in up to that date. He liked guns and liked firing them. Beating someone to death with one seems out of character, but obviously he could not be discounted until the right questions had been asked. Unfortunately, that opportunity never arose: Topliss was shot dead during a gun battle with police in June 1920. From that point on, it's fair to say the investigation fizzled away to nothing and the case was eventually left on the unsolved pile.

The mystery for me has always been why Florence was killed in this way. Various writers have suggested the crime could not have been premeditated because there were two women sat in that carriage when the killer entered the compartment. In other words, he could not have intended murder when he climbed aboard that train. They suggest the murder was opportunistic and carried out during a robbery gone wrong. But that cannot be the case. Being on a train, alone in a carriage with the victim, and knowing the train would not stop until Lewes, to my mind shows that murder had always been intended. There could have been no successful robbery if the victim was left alive to build a description of her attacker for local police: the chance of arrest was too great. Besides, how did the killer know the woman in the third-class compartment carried jewellery? I tend to believe the robbery was intentional, if there ever was a robbery, as was the murder. Why this was so is probably what baffled police and everyone else who has looked at this case.

Could Mabel have been the murderer? It may sound outlandish, but is not impossible. The robbery only takes place if she is telling the truth about the jewellery. The man in the brown suit only gets into the carriage if she really saw him. And why did the man whom Henry Duck saw leave the carriage at Lewes not match Mabel's description? On the day prior to that fateful train journey, Florence had spent the day with her only living relative in Britain, her aunt, Baroness Farina, at Tonbridge. Why did she not stay overnight and travel to St Leonards from there? Why travel back to London, only to set off again the following day? As far as I can see this distance away from the murder, these questions were neither asked nor answered. Newspaper reports at the time suggested there had been a struggle in the compartment, possibly because they found it difficult to accept that a woman could be murdered in cold blood, on a train, whilst simply reading a book, for a few trinkets of jewellery. They also suggested a sexual motive, but there is absolutely no evidence in support of that supposition. The evidence suggests it was exactly as portrayed in the Coroner's court. Florence Nightingale Shore did not have a chance to fight back. She was murdered whilst seated and probably reading, without provocation and probably not for financial gain. There were no clues, no evidence and no real motive (robbery, though suspected, was never satisfactorily proven), which is no doubt why it has remained unsolved for almost 100 years.

## Chapter 10

# The Burning Car Mystery

*The murder of Evelyn Foster, 1931*

T he village of Otterburn, 15 miles on the English side of the Scottish border and some 30 miles north-west of Newcastle, sits inside the Northumberland National Park. Hexham is its nearest neighbour, and in the 1930s its main road link was the Jedburgh to Newcastle road. Picturesque in summer, the surrounding landscape is often bleak and snowbound in winter. Otterburn Woollen Mill, which sat on the edge of the village, was once its key employer, producing fine rugs and blankets throughout the nineteenth century and building a reputation in the first quarter of the twentieth century for the manufacture of quality tweed cloth. Relatively self-sufficient, the village handled produce and livestock from the outlying farms and had its own school, offering education from infant through to senior levels. As part of the early tourist trail, it also had the historical battle site of Otterburn (1388), along with its tower, which brought visitors into the village en route to the Scottish border towns. The old coaching Inn, The Percy Arms, was able to provide the necessary sustenance to any that needed it.

By the start of the 1930s, the village was a relatively prosperous place with employment readily accessible to locals. A number of small businesses had formed within its boundaries after the First World War, with access being provided by the local bus service operated by Joseph Foster from his garage, which employed its own mechanics for ongoing maintenance and repair. He helped keep the village moving whilst his daughter, Evelyn, operated the only local taxi service. It was an extremely successful partnership. At 27-years-old, Evelyn was financially independent. Still single, and seemingly quite content to remain so, she had built a viable, thriving business alongside her father. Trade came to her from both locals and those living in the outlying villages. Earnings were perhaps capped somewhat by location and unpredictable weather, but not significantly so. For her the work was easy: she liked the driving, her fares and the travel.

People, she found, were always engaging and usually accommodating. That all changed in January 1931.

On the 6th of that month, Evelyn had a fare from Otterburn to Rochester, a small village some 5 miles along the Jedburgh road. What happened from that point on has baffled and confused people ever since. It is a story pieced together from a series of confusing statements she made to her mother during that night and the early hours of 7 January as she lay dying. It is a muddled, perplexing account of her own murder, told piecemeal and recorded in part by police, who were only present for a brief time, or recalled later by others whose memories of the events often differed.

Putting together these differing strands into a cohesive account, as presented at the later inquest, it appeared that after leaving Rochester and travelling back to Otterburn, Evelyn was flagged down by a man stood beside a parked car in the tiny hamlet of Elishaw. She heard him thank the car's occupants for giving him a lift before he walked over and asked if she could take him to Otterburn. She agreed; common courtesy demanded it. The other car then drove off in the direction of Hexham. Once in the passenger seat, he told her they had brought him south from Jedburgh and he hoped to catch a bus to Newcastle. Obviously familiar with the local bus service, Evelyn told him he had already missed the last bus but offered to take him as a paying fare as far as Ponteland, where there was a late service; apparently there was then some discussion about the cost. She quoted a £2 fare but told him she would have to stop off first at the garage in Otterburn for petrol. The car had a two-gallon can in the back in case of emergency, but she wanted to avoid having to use it. While perhaps expensive, he raised no real objection, just asking that she drop him in the village whilst she went to refill. She thought he wanted to nose around, to see if anyone else was about and travelling the same way, a free lift being better than a taxi ride. They agreed to meet again outside the Percy Arms Hotel in the centre of the village if he had no luck elsewhere.

According to her mother, she got back to the house at about 7.00 pm. She explained about the man she had picked up on her return from Rochester, describing him as being well dressed, wearing a bowler hat and being well spoken: 'He looked respectable and gentlemanly and a kind of a nut [or knut, as reported].'

At the time, her sister, Dorothy, was in the house and suggested she go to find George Philipson and take him along for the ride, perhaps as a little added safety. It seems the Fosters preferred Evelyn to have a man with her if she worked at night. George was a trusted friend and worked for the business, and they possibly even harboured thoughts that one day he would become a part of the family. Whether Evelyn felt the same is not known, but it would appear she never sought him out. After filling the car with petrol, she left the garage alone. The time was around 7.15 pm. Minutes later, she collected the stranger from outside the Percy Arms and set out on the Newcastle road for Ponteland.

For the first 10 or so miles there was polite conversation. He smoked a lot of cigarettes, told her a little about himself, that he knew the Midlands well but not the North-East, but said nothing about his life, work, past or family. However, as the car reached the village of Belsay there was an argument; about what is not known. He demanded control of the car and she objected. He was insistent, slid across the seat and grabbed the steering wheel, forcing her back against the driver's door. A bench seat at the front of the car with a low back meant that she possibly clambered over it at that point and climbed into the back. There she probably stayed whilst he turned the car around, drove back toward Otterburn and eventually pulled over at a place known locally as Wolf's Nick, located about 4 miles south of the village. Why he stopped there has never been established, and from that point on the story becomes a little vague and uncertain. From the little that Evelyn said, it would appear she had, by this time, returned to the front of the car and sat as a passenger. There was banter, relatively light-hearted, and he offered her a cigarette, which she declined, being a non-smoker. Then things changed rapidly. Strong words were exchanged and he struck her, perhaps more than once, according to her fragmented account. Somehow, possibly to escape the violence, she ended up on the back seat a second time. What happened next is as contentious as it is controversial.

Evelyn's mother presumed the worst. Unlike today, to ask probing questions of a sexual nature was unheard of in 1931, the term 'rape' being rarely used. So when Mrs Foster questioned her daughter, she skirted around the subject and posed her question in a manner she believed her daughter would better understand: 'Did he interfere with you?' Evelyn said he had. To Mrs Foster, at that moment, her answer meant she had been raped. It would appear that, realizing the impact of that admission on her mother, Evelyn then added that she had fought for her life.

True or not, from that point on the story becomes unclear. Evelyn recounted that she lost consciousness for a time and was left in the back of the car. She vaguely remembered a blanket, coat or some sort of rug being thrown over her. The man apparently leaned into the back, took a bottle or tin from his pocket and threw its contents on to her. She remembered nothing else until she was jolted awake by the car travelling over rough ground and being on fire. The car came to a halt some 70 yards from the road, on moorland. With considerable effort, she struggled out of the back and, severely burned, managed to crawl away onto the moor, the car by now well ablaze. Confused and understandably disorientated, she believed she heard the petrol tank explode, the sound of a whistle and a car driving away on the road, which was now above where she lay.

She was found at 10.00 pm that night by Cecil Johnson, driver of the returning Newcastle to Otterburn bus. The fire was almost out by this time, just low flames and smoke which had attracted his attention. Along with his conductor, 15-year-old Thomas Rutherford, he found Evelyn barely breathing, lying out in the open, licking at ice that had formed on the grass. Most of her clothing from the neck down had been destroyed by the fire, her face was burnt, blackened and bruised, and she had some sort of wound at the back of her head. But her hair had been untouched, perhaps because, it transpired later, she had been wearing a hat (which was never found). Between them, they carried her to the bus and then drove her back to the Fosters' home, The Kennels, where her parents, initially not realizing the extent of her injuries, managed to get her indoors and upstairs.

This was a rural area, with no doctor and no nearby hospital, but the village did have a district nurse. The bus was quickly turned around and sent off to find her. It took a while, but eventually Cecil Johnson tracked her down and managed to get her back to the house to begin whatever First Aid she could. In the meantime, Evelyn's father, Joseph, made a phone call to the police and his own GP in nearby Bellingham some 8 miles away. Doctor Eachran arrived at the house some half an hour later, along with police officers. It was a forlorn hope from the outset. The moment he saw the extent of the burns, the doctor realized Evelyn had no hope of survival. So severe were they around her waist and lower extremities that all he could do was try to keep her comfortable and pain-free. She died around 8.30 am the following morning.

Back at the scene of the fire, another confused picture was emerging concerning the state of the vehicle when it was found and just how destructive that fire had been. Police Constable William Turnbull was sent to guard it some eight hours after Evelyn's rescue. When he arrived, the scene was quiet, still in darkness and not visible from the road, which had obviously kept sightseers away. But he did not remain alone for long. Others joined him just after daybreak, including PC Ferguson, who had been at the Foster house, and PC Proud. It was their later testimony that was key to trying to understand exactly what had happened when the fire started. There was no effective police protocol in 1931 when it came to isolating a crime scene, as officers would do today. So, as others joined them, things were moved, touched, handled and examined. The crime scene was effectively contaminated, albeit inadvertently, by those carrying out the investigation, plus a few well-meaning visitors to the site, which rendered any resulting testimony unreliable. Nevertheless, it still formed the basis of the developing police enquiry.

The recorded and accepted crime scene report is of a four-door Hudson car, burnt out from the inside. All the leather seating was burnt away, but the engine was undamaged and clearly was not the source of the fire. The two doors on the off-side (driver and passenger) were open. An empty petrol can was seen at some point still in the back of the car, but at another point lying on its side behind the car, with its screw cap discarded a few feet away. A small glass bottle some feet away from the back wheels was subsequently found to have contained a soft drink. A burnt woman's purse containing money was near to the back wheel on the driver's side. There was no burnt grass or heather, and the car was still in gear. There was also fire damage to part of the bonnet, the windscreen was broken and the car's petrol tank was still intact (there had been no explosion).

From this scenario, police had to try to better understand what had happened to Evelyn Foster when she had been attacked, and how the fire had started. It was an impossible task from the outset. Forensic fire investigation was in its infancy in 1931, and any knowledge previously gleaned from examining a scene such as this was not available to Northumberland police. For Chief Constable Captain James Fullarton, who had control of the investigation, this was simply going to be a manhunt based around the bits of description Evelyn had managed to pass on prior to her death.

For his officers, that was never going to be easy. The Northumberland force had limited access to cars; there were a few motorbikes and lots of bicycles. Fortunately, they did have reasonable telephone links with other police forces, so, by late morning on 7 January, most forces across the north of England and southern Scotland had received details of the murder and a vague description of the assailant. That assailant, as far as local police were concerned, was the man Evelyn had given the lift to on the night of her death. They decided, therefore, to centre their search on the car that had brought him south from Jedburgh. By late morning they had received information that a car travelling south, containing three men, had been seen during the late afternoon of the killing and had stopped at the Redesdale Arms near Otterburn.

They concentrated on this particular vehicle despite there having been information flowing into police stations concerning others. Deciding this was the most likely vehicle to have deposited the stranger at Elishaw, police made a public appeal through the BBC for information. It was broadcast on 7 January and carried by all national newspapers:

'At 10.30 pm, January 6, a young woman named Foster, driver of a hackney car, was found burned near the car off the highway south of Otterburn, Northumberland, in a very injured condition, and has since died. The Police are anxious to trace a four-seater, closed, dark coloured car, index mark T N, with a number consisting of four figures, the last figure or figure but one being a two. The car was described as possibly an Essex and had left the Redesdale Hotel, near Otterburn, Northumberland, about 7pm with three men of the following description:

1. About 38, 5ft 8ins, short dark moustache, very bad teeth, dark hair, smartly dressed.
2. About 40, 5ft 5ins, broad face, prominent cheek bones, very bad teeth, practically non in top jaw, wearing slate coloured suit, no overcoat, no hat, badly in need of a shave.
3. About 30, 5ft 7ins, well built, blue overcoat, no hat.

Had all travelled possibly from Jedburgh believed headed for London.'

The 'TN' index mark identified the car as being registered in Tyneside, as was Evelyn's. Whilst they waited for the public at large to respond, the inquest opened on 8 January but was almost immediately adjourned until February. The post-mortem and other enquiries were obviously ongoing, and time was needed before any logical conclusions could be reached.

The appeal and subsequent follow-up articles and accounts of the murder, in both national and local newspapers, created a huge interest in the crime. Numerous sightings of possible suspects caused an upsurge in police activity, not just in Northumberland but across much of the country. However, it never located the three men sought and, as time passed, it also became clear that these three were perhaps not the right men after all. Other cars had been seen on the Newcastle to Jedburgh road that night.

It is probably fair to say that the investigating officers found them all. The exception was the car that Evelyn had claimed had dropped off her eventual passenger; crucially that had not been found. Supposed to have been heading to Hexham, it was never located. There was speculation at the time that the driver was a woman, which ought to have made the search easier, there being fewer women drivers than men in 1931, but that was never really proven. But it does strongly suggest that perhaps the police and press had been trying to locate men who had no involvement at all in Evelyn's murder, and a car that may not have even existed. This was a search mounted on tenuous, vague and perhaps even misleading information provided by a woman in significant pain and on the edge of death, not, as was usual, based on information received via a legal written statement – something Evelyn never managed to do. Everything done in the early stages of their investigation was based on a conversation between mother and daughter in the presence of family and occasionally police officers. Given these circumstances, it is perhaps understandable that the Northumberland force were, to some extent, always grasping at straws.

Nonetheless, what they did do was effective, even if it did not move the investigation forward in the way they would have perhaps expected. With the certain knowledge that Evelyn had been at home and had filled her car with petrol between 7.00 pm and 7.15 pm, they had mounted a search to find any villagers on the street that night. The hope was that a stranger would have been instantly noticed. They found most people who had been around, but unfortunately, none who saw the man Evelyn collected as a fare. They also found the drivers of a number of cars on the roads around Otterburn and travelling to or from Belsay. None had seen Evelyn or her passenger. In addition to all that diligent police work, they also managed to find the driver of a car who saw the fire but did not stop. He had not realized the seriousness of the situation, but crucially had not passed any stranger on the road. The police had also tried to understand just how the car had left the road and ended up on the moor, but had struggled to make sense of Evelyn's account and were still uncertain at the end of their deliberations as to whether it had been driven off the road or had been left driverless. Neither were they certain as to how the fire had started and exactly who had caused it. Doubts, it seems, had even begun to emerge over the veracity of her account, and by the middle of the month the investigation was beginning to flounder. Chief Constable Fullarton started to voice concern over the lack of supporting evidence, which he had expected his officers to have found, despite limited resources.

When the inquest resumed on Monday, 2 February, even the newspapers were beginning to question the accuracy of the information they had been receiving. Coverage began to fall away as progress failed to develop. The Foster family challenged what they saw as a police failure to mount a cohesive murder enquiry. The lack of suspects was obviously paramount, but perhaps more disturbing was this change of attitude from the chief constable. The family were to find little solace in the court.

Coroner Mr Philip Dodds opened proceedings in Otterburn's Memorial Hall. The weekend had seen heavy snow, with blizzards blowing for the best part of two days, which had forced the closure of the road to Newcastle. Travel around the area was hazardous at best, making attendance difficult and restricting press coverage, but enough had navigated a way through the snow to fill the room.

Essentially, this was a play in three acts: the family, the investigation and the pathology. The testimony was spread over three intense days. For Evelyn's family, particularly her mother, it was an endurance test. The lack of any valid written statement taken before Evelyn's death had placed her mother in the role of key witness. It was therefore inevitable that the court looked to her to explain again the circumstances of her daughter's death and the events of the night of 6 January. As the first witness called, she was questioned throughout much of that first morning by the coroner. For her, nothing had changed over the intervening month since Evelyn's death. Her recall had not been affected by time and she told her story with a deal of clarity. However, this was a legal stage, and once the coroner had elicited as much information as he thought relevant for the jury to hear, she was cross-examined by the Northumberland Police's legal team. Their intention seems to have been to challenge the meaning behind a certain aspect of Mrs Foster's statement. The chief constable had, by this time, already expressed strong doubts about exactly what had happened to Evelyn Foster. He also had access to information the Foster family did not. It would appear his intention was to discredit, in part, the statement she had made to the court. Sexual assault and rape was the cornerstone of the police investigation, and they believed from the outset it had been the cause of the stranger's attack and the subsequent burning of both Evelyn and the car. But this was built upon Mrs Foster's interpretation of her daughter's answer to that one ambiguous question: 'Did he interfere with you?' Doubts had arisen in police ranks that when Evelyn said 'yes', she had not meant rape, or outrage, as it was termed at the time. That was construed by her mother because it had been her own understanding of the term 'interfere', but had not necessarily been that of her daughter. If that were the case, as far as police were concerned, the murder itself became suspect. So too did the rest of Evelyn's dying deposition. An obdurate Mrs Foster refused to countenance any misunderstanding, certain that Evelyn had known full well the meaning behind the question and would not have deliberately misled her in her answer. She was wrong.

After hearing from other members of the Foster family, none of whom had the impact of Margaret Foster, a variety of witnesses were brought to the court over the next twenty-four hours. These included motorists who had travelled on the relevant day, locals who had seen Evelyn's car in the early part of that night – including one of the fares whom she had taken to Rochester before returning home – and those who had seen or passed the fire on the moor. There were no witnesses who had seen a stranger.

The coroner then heard the first of two pieces of scientific testimony. The first was from Professor Stuart McDonald, Dean of the University of Durham College of Medicine at Newcastle. He had conducted the post-mortem, the results of which were no doubt passed to the chief constable long before the inquest opened, which may explain his later change in attitude. His evidence to the court was damning as far as the investigation was concerned and in direct conflict with Mrs Foster's earlier key testimony. Evelyn Foster, he told the coroner, had not been raped; he had found no sign of sexual activity or interference. As far as his examinations were concerned, Evelyn had never had intercourse, either that night or at any time earlier. She was still a virgin. Neither had he found any clear indication that she had suffered violence against her person, with no bruises, cuts or abrasions. However, he did admit under questioning that the extensive burns to her skin had made that conclusion a little questionable. Nevertheless, his testimony, based on his own factual report, was damning as far as the Foster family were concerned. It also led the coroner to raise the possibility that Evelyn could have killed herself by accident. He intimated as much when he raised the possibility with the professor that she could have poured the petrol over the back of the car, and accidentally being caught up in the resultant fire. Perhaps this was a thought that had also crossed the chief constable's mind.

The second piece of analysis, in many ways supporting this new evolving theory, came from a Professor Dunn. He had examined stains found at the scene, some of which were thought to have been of blood, and also the remains of Evelyn's clothing. But the stains, which would have supported the violent attack suggested by Evelyn, were found to have been made by some other substance. No blood staining had been discovered in or around the car. On the other hand, he had been able to confirm that the clothes, which were known to have been expensively purchased, had been in contact with petrol, though just how and where, he had been unable to show as not enough of them had remained to produce any significant result.

In his final summation to the jury, Coroner Dodds had clearly reached his own conclusion that no murder had taken place, and effectively instructed them to return a verdict that would reflect the view that Evelyn had been the author of her downfall. After hearing all the testimony, he appeared satisfied that it was most likely she had caused the fire herself; possibly, he argued, for insurance. The car had a value and was insured through Joseph Foster's company. He considered it possible she had leaned into the car, poured petrol onto the back seats and tragically set herself alight. The stranger was perhaps a figment of her own imagination. The story told to her mother, fragmented as it was, was invented to try and hide the facts. But this was a jury made up of people who knew the Foster family and held Evelyn in some regard. Whilst some of the evidence conflicted with events as related by Evelyn's mother, they still accepted her account as being truthful. It took the best part of a couple of hours, but they were eventually unanimous in their verdict: Evelyn had not caused her own injuries and she had been murdered.

For Chief Constable Fullarton and the coroner alike, the verdict was a blow they had not expected. The investigation was already in the process of being wound down. Senior officers in the police had thought for several days the investigation would be brought to a halt, and had probably planned accordingly. Having heard all the evidence for both parties, it had probably seemed relatively clear-cut: no witnesses to the event, no existence of a stranger, no corroborating scientific or pathological evidence and a statement that appeared more hearsay than fact. They believed there was enough there to call off the enquiry and move on to something else.

But was that fair? Joseph Foster definitely thought not. He knew well enough that the police, through their chief constable, did not believe his daughter. But he did. On 9 February, dissatisfied with Captain James Fullarton's handling of the whole affair, he wrote a letter to the Home Secretary, John Robert Clynes. In this letter, which was widely publicized, he claimed Northumberland's chief constable had held an interview with a newspaper reporter in which he had objected to the inquest jury's verdict, claiming it was against the weight of evidence. He also raised three questions:

> 'Was my daughter's burned car left unprotected for hours so that fingerprints could not be taken?
> Is it a fact that the police made no attempt to check footprints on the scene of the tragedy until the ground had been trampled over by curious sightseers?
> 'Why was the skill and experience of Scotland Yard ignored by the Northumberland police?'

Clearly, relationships and communication had broken down. The Home Secretary responded at the end of February, though not with answers. Those, he claimed, must come from the Northumberland Joint Committee, effectively the chief constable's employer. Their response followed in March, perhaps not surprisingly in support of the beleaguered head of police and stating that the conversation with the press had not been intentional. As for Mr Foster's questions, they were probably easily answered. The weather had obviously played a significant part and the car was on moorland, making it difficult, I would have thought, to obtain footprints, and fire apparently destroyed any fingerprint evidence. As for Scotland Yard, they were only ever called in if murder was verified and local police unable to handle it. In the case of Evelyn Foster, because the chief constable had doubts, I would imagine he saw no point in calling in the so-called experts.

That is not a defence of Chief Constable Fullarton's attitude or approach. My feelings are that Evelyn was certainly murdered and that he should have mounted a better and more thorough investigation of the events of 6 January 1931. But once the post-mortem results had become public, the reason for continuing the investigation was obviously compromised. In Diane Jane's excellent book, *Death at Wolf's Nick*, she examines this case in great detail, having had access to the police files, which had remained closed for many years. She mounts a strong case against Captain James Fullarton and his eventual inertia, and a forceful argument in support of the jury's verdict; all of whom, as far as I can see, never regretted their justified decision in support of the Foster family.

So who did kill Evelyn? There have been a number of candidates put forward over the years, and I have no doubt others will eventually arrive on the scene. As for myself, I have no real candidate. The case is a confusing mix of fact and fiction created by Evelyn Foster's deathbed statement.

Regarding the theory it was a sexual attack resulting in a rape gone wrong, the pathology clearly demonstrated that had not been the case, which destroyed the motive for murder as far as the police were concerned at the time. It also casts doubt over the veracity of Evelyn's account of events on that night, as interpreted by her mother, but it does not automatically declare the account to have been a fabrication. Margaret Foster's term 'interfered with' obviously had a different meaning for mother and daughter. I believe Evelyn did not understand it to mean she had been raped, or 'outraged', as it was generally referred to in 1931; rather that she had been touched inappropriately, as modern parlance would term it. So when she reacted positively to her mother's question, she was being truthful as she saw it. Therefore, what she said happened that night has to have been true. A man, her taxi fare, had attacked her and had made a sexual approach. She had fought him off and he had deliberately struck her.

Who this man was has been the puzzle ever since. Police accepted that he had to have been a stranger to the area, probably English, possibly living south of Newcastle, maybe the Midlands. They mounted a reasonably comprehensive search involving more than one police force. They successfully tracked down drivers on the road that night and locals moving around the various villages, none of whom were able to offer any clue to this stranger's identity. In turn, when this negative result combined with the post-mortem evidence had been made known, they had decided the whole affair to be untrue, a fraudulent version of events to cover up a potential false insurance claim.

That is abject nonsense. Evelyn's appalling injuries speak for themselves. Someone had murdered her that night in January, and possibly escaped simply because the police looked in the wrong place. The so-called stranger was only that because the investigating team believed it to be so. But what if he had been in plain sight the whole time? There are aspects of this crime that suggest the man Evelyn picked up that night lived much nearer to Otterburn than was thought. It is also not beyond the realms of possibility that she knew him or knew of him, had seen him before, but perhaps did not know his name or where he came from.

Is it not also possible that this was a man she did not want her parents to meet? A man perhaps they would have disapproved of, which is why he was dropped in the village when she returned home. Also, why fill up with petrol if you were unsure your fare would still be waiting to be picked up? Surely you would only do so if you were certain of making the trip. And where did he go for some twenty-five minutes or so?

My suspicion is that there was perhaps some sort of familiarity. She picked him up as planned from the Percy Arms and drove down to Belsay. Once there, they had some sort of an argument. He took control of the car – exactly how is debatable – turned it around, drove back toward Otterburn and stopped at Wolf's Nick. There, they talked. She would have been sat beside him in the front of the car. From what we know, that conversation was friendly, not hostile. However, things changed, and he made a clumsy sexual advance which she rebuffed. He persisted, so she got out of the car. He followed. They argued, maybe even fought out in the road, and he tried to force her into the back of the car. When she continued to refuse, he hit her, hard, on the side of her face. It knocked her out and he thought he had killed her. So he bundled her into the back and panicked. At that point he had two choices. If he lived Newcastle way, he could have thrown her body onto the moor, turned the car around and driven away. In 1931, it is doubtful he would ever have been stopped. But if he lived reasonably locally and knew exactly where he was, he could drive the car onto the moorland. There he could dowse it in petrol to destroy his fingerprints and the body. He chose the latter. But Evelyn was not dead, something perhaps he did not realize until the following day.

The idea is not without merit. The car was found in gear, which suggests it was driven on to the moor. It was January, cold and particularly dark. Driving onto rough moorland has inherent dangers unless you are aware that the land does not slope away too steeply. It would seem the driver knew that. Evelyn, in her fragmented statement, also makes it clear she was not aware of what was happening around her or that she was on fire until it was too late. Neither did she see her attacker leave the scene of the fire, which would suggest the idea her killer thought she was already dead is not necessarily fatuous. The return journey from Belsay, which had he lived miles away to the south makes little sense, is also suggestive of a man on familiar turf, someone aware of his surroundings and a man able to drive a car. A rare thing in 1931. Most people would only ever have used public transport or walked. Owning a car was expensive. So Evelyn's killer was probably in a reasonably well-paid occupation. The bowler hat which he supposedly wore and his acceptance of a £2 fare (£95 today) were an indication of a man well-disposed financially. If he had been otherwise, would he not have stolen her money that night? Her purse was found intact with money still inside beside the burnt-out car. He was also not afraid of the car being found. Setting fire to a vehicle at that time of night was effectively lighting a beacon that would be seen for miles around, if there was anyone to see it. But at Wolf's Nick there was no-one to see it; just a bend in the road, with Otterburn to the north and Kirkwhelpington to the south, and no inhabited buildings anywhere nearby. In many ways it was the perfect spot to carry out a murder, light a bonfire and walk away unseen.

Whoever the murderer was, he has Chief Constable Captain James Fullarton to thank for his escape. Though I have some sympathy for the position he found himself in, the decision not to call in Scotland Yard when he had the chance was clearly a mistake. But there is no certainty that they would have fared any better than he did. The murder was always going to be difficult to solve from the moment Professor McDonald stunned the Coroner's court with the pronouncement that Evelyn had not been raped. However, the Northumberland Police's investigation failed not simply because of that, but because they could only accept murder as a result of rape. However, sexual assault, as we know today, takes many forms. Evelyn Foster deserved better. Her murder ought to have been more thoroughly investigated, not questioned. Perhaps if that had been the case it would not still sit today on the unsolved pile.

## Chapter 11

# A Case of Ballistics

*The Murder of Doctor Angelos Zemenides, 1933*

Twenty-year-old Theodosius Petrou arrived in London from Cyprus in November 1931. Annexed by Britain at the start of the First World War in 1914, after the Ottoman Empire had allied itself to Germany, Cyprus had been declared a Crown Colony in 1925. It was essentially a country divided by both religion and nationality. The Greek faction wanted union with Greece (Enosis), the Turkish faction wanted partition; whilst Britain appeared to favour neither. This resulted in riots, the worst of which manifested in the capital, Nicosia, in 1931, causing the destruction of Britain's Government House. For people living through this turmoil, life was, understandably, hard and finances difficult to maintain. Families looked elsewhere to subsidise meagre wages and help maintain their own local industries. For Petrou's family back home on the island, whatever he could earn in Britain would help them pay outstanding mortgages on the land they held, which in 1933 meant a debt value of around £4,000 (£200,000 today).

He moved into London's Cypriot society, who helped secure him work as a pastry chef in a popular Piccadilly restaurant almost as soon as he disembarked, presumably brought about by contacts and an existing skill. That led in turn to an introduction to the Greek Cypriot Brotherhood, an organization founded by Cypriots to help new immigrants. Their aim was to provide access to English language classes and provide cultural and educational assistance along with moral support. For Theodosius Petrou, at that period of his life, it was probably a godsend and he used their resources throughout the early summer of 1932, meeting, through them, Doctor Angelos Zemenides. Exactly how they met is not known, but what they discussed when they met is. The doctor, who spoke very good English, taught the language to new arrivals and, when required, worked as an interpreter for London Police, a useful sideline. At least that is how the doctor viewed it. He could also arrange marriages, telling Petrou that for a fee he could arrange for him to meet a woman whose family would pay a £200 dowry for her marriage. This was money, he convinced Petrou, that he could send back to Cyprus to enable his parents to clear their debts. Whether gullible or simply because he felt lonely, Petrou paid the doctor £13 (£595 by today's valuation), £10 of which he had to borrow. But Doctor Zemenides was no matchmaker. There were a few introductions, but Petrou felt the women he was asked to meet were not the marrying kind. By the end of summer, dissatisfied, he asked for his money to be returned. However, Zemenides was in no mood to start giving refunds. He told Petrou the money had been spent, but Petrou was not so easily dissuaded and persisted with his demands over the following weeks, hounding the doctor at every opportunity and discussing the poor return on his investment with any who would listen. He eventually forced Zemenides to offer a compromise. The two men met again before Christmas. The doctor pleaded poverty and offered £4, which Petrou accepted, but with the expectation the remaining £9 would follow on at some undefined date in the near future. Whether he really expected that balance to be forthcoming is doubtful. Nonetheless, through the early winter he still held out expectations that the doctor would honour the debt. He discussed it with his old landlady, Florence Marriott, around Christmas time, though her view differed somewhat from his own.

Not that the debt seemed to have made any significant impact on Doctor Zemenides. Well-liked amongst many in the Cypriot community living in London – though not all – his language services were in constant demand. Multi-lingual, he had moved to the capital around 1925, and since then had worked solely with new immigrants, not always of Greek origin. Teaching English to adults at a school in London's Long Acre, and being occasionally paid for private tuition, were the greatest call on his time. Through his association with the Greek Brotherhood and the London police's need of his interpreting skills, he had enhanced his reputation amongst certain quarters of the Cypriot community. In turn that helped finance lodgings on Upper Park Road, Hampstead, a large house populated by foreign students, where he was also involved in the day-to-day issues and problems of up to fifty young people; visits to the doctor, dentist, hospital or helping translate letters and understand bus timetables being the most common. Somewhere within that community he had created enemies, and on 2 January 1933, they struck.

At 11.20 pm that night, mining engineer Arthur Deby, who rented a downstairs room in the same house as Doctor Zemenides, opened the front door to a man asking if the doctor would see him. Well used to late-night callers, Deby invited the man into the hallway. They spoke together briefly, then Deby ran upstairs to the doctor's room. The visitor followed. When Zemenides answered the door, Deby returned downstairs and left the two talking together in a language he did not understand. Within minutes, Deby heard the doctor call out: 'Mr Deby, Mr Deby, quick, quick, help me.'

Deby ran out into the hallway and found the two men struggling together at the bottom of the stairs. The stranger had a gun, described later as a revolver, in his right hand. Deby shouted at them to stop. Doctor Zemenides broke away and the stranger fired at him. The bullet missed. Zemenides then managed to get behind Deby, who was trying to usher him into his own room, pushing him back behind the open door. But the stranger fired a second shot, then ran out of the house. The bullet struck Zemenides in the back of the left shoulder. He was dead by the time his body hit the ground.

Within twenty-four hours of examining the scene, police were pointing a finger at Petrou, guided toward him, no doubt, by those who knew of the dispute over the doctor's failed attempt to find him a bride. On 4 January, he was in custody at Tottenham Court Road police station and stood in an identity parade on the same day. He was released shortly afterwards when Mr Deby, who had seen and spoken to the killer, failed to pick him out of the line-up. But his freedom was not about to last long. On the following day, Aristoteles Christodolous, owner of a restaurant on Union Street, told police that he had once owned a gun. The weapon was a revolver and he had sold it to Petrou for £3 on 29 or 30 December, along with seven bullets. Petrou, he claimed, had wanted to buy it for a friend in Cyprus and intended to post it back home. The same day, West End bar owner Page Hall told police he had seen Petrou the day after the killing. They had discussed the money he paid for the bride that never arrived, and in that same conversation the Greek Cypriot had admitted to the murder. For Detective Inspector Sands, therefore, when Petrou walked back into the police station that same day to ask if he could help further, it was case closed. He had him immediately detained and organized a search of his rooms in Clerkenwell. There, in the cellar, hidden behind a bag placed on top of the coal bin, he found a gun, still loaded, but with only five cartridges. Petrou was duly charged with murder. According to his later statement, the gun had not belonged to him and he had never purchased one. It was, he insisted, a set-up; either by the police or by someone in the Greek community who needed him to take the blame for a killing they had carried out.

There is no doubt, and Detective Inspector Sands was well aware, that Doctor Zemenides had enemies. A number of Cypriots living in London at the time were incensed by his willingness to work as an interpreter in trials involving men from their community. Anger tended to centre around the murder trial in 1931 of Alexander Anastassiou, a 23-year-old who had been accused of murdering waitress Evelyn Holt in his rooms in Warren Street, just off Tottenham Court Road. The trial had revolved around whether he had killed her in self-defence, as he had claimed, or deliberately murdered her. It was certainly a difficult case for the jury, who, having heard all the evidence, were given the choice of returning a verdict of manslaughter or murder. They chose to convict on the latter, and Anastassiou was executed at Pentonville on 3 June 1931. To many this was a miscarriage of justice. A number of people must have known the man and just how volatile his relationship had been with Holt, a woman shown during the trial to have been extremely jealous, argumentative and demanding. Yet why criticism should have been levelled at the doctor seems somewhat bizarre. There was also the possibility that Zemenides had 'a past', nothing to do with his police work but something left behind on Cyprus years before and long forgotten. Perhaps there had been a vendetta or some long-standing feud, which had brought a killer to London or had caused a killer to be hired. Melodramatic though this might seem, it was not totally impossible and was something the police were all too well aware could have happened within that community, but were never able to substantiate. That is, in fact, if they ever really explored the possibility with due diligence. Discovery of the gun on Petrou's premises seemed conclusive, and understandably so. For Detective Inspector Sands, despite the key witness to the killing, Mr Deby, failing to identify Petrou in a line-up, it was enough to charge him with murder.

The trial opened on 14 March at the Old Bailey before Mr Justice Humphreys. It was, essentially, a straightforward prosecution. The Crown case, delivered by Eustace Fulton – who had been involved in what had become known as the Royal Mail case in 1931, which had changed the ways British companies would be audited – centred around Petrou's failed marriage arrangement. That alone, argued the prosecution, had caused him to harbour a grudge. Failure to force Doctor Zemenides to refund his money had then set in motion a series of actions: purchasing a gun, locating the doctor's home and finally carrying out an execution, all designed to satisfy honour or exact revenge, or both. The argument was credible, and up to a point was backed by strong evidential support. But for the prosecution to succeed, it also had to have been the gun that police recovered from Petrou's home that had fired the shots. Here their case floundered.

From the outset, the defence never really contested the fact that the relationship between Petrou and Doctor Zemenides had soured during the summer and autumn of 1932. Too much evidence existed to strongly suggest that was the case, which of course created motive. However, what the defence had discovered was the science of ballistics. They engaged Major Sir Gerald Burrard to examine the bullets recovered from both the body and the murder scene. An expert in firearms, Major Burrard understood in detail just how every gun left unique marks on every bullet it fired, with no two guns ever leaving identical marks. To assist in his examination, Major Burrard brought in renowned handgun expert Doctor R.K. Wilson. Between the two of them they were able to show that the gun recovered, a .32 self-loading Browning pistol, had held two standard self-loading pistol cartridges, rimless with nickel–jacketed bullets, and three .32 revolver cartridges with the rims filed off (which made them fit), and with lead bullets.

The bullet extracted from the body of Doctor Zemenides was a nickel-jacketed bullet, and that recovered buried in a skirting board at the scene a .32 revolver lead bullet. Both recovered bullets, according to their expert view, could have been fired from the gun found in the cellar, but close examination showed that not to be the case. Striation markings on the recovered bullets showed they were fired from the same calibre weapon, but from a different gun.

The defence conclusion, therefore, was that someone else had killed the doctor and had used a different gun, but the same calibre of bullet. The 'wrong' gun, so to speak, had then been placed in Petrou's property for police to find, the real killer obviously unaware that ballistics were advanced enough to match a bullet to a gun so precisely. It was a fortunate mistake and one that saved Theodosius Petrou from the noose, the jury eventually returning a 'not guilty' verdict.

So who did kill Doctor Angelos Zemenides? It was probably a man who had arrived back in Cyprus by the time the trial opened; someone who had been helped by others in the London Cypriot community, and someone possibly paid to carry out the killing. It was done possibly because of the doctor's aid and assistance to police through his interpreting work, though exactly why will never now be known.

*Chapter 12*

# The Country Estate Murders

*The murders of George and Lillian Peach, 1952*

The picturesque village of Ashton, virtually untouched by time, sits today as it has for over 100 years. It is a testimony to its architect, William Huckvale, who in 1912 was brought to Northamptonshire by the Hon. Charles Rothschild to design an Edwardian village for the workers employed on the Rothschilds' Ashton Wold estate. Nestling in the eastern corner of the county, it is some 20 miles from Northampton, with the historic town of Oundle as its nearest neighbour. The village consisted of only thirty-two cottages. Surrounded by over 5,000 acres of arable farming land, it was responsible during the Second World War for producing a decent portion of the country's food needs through the growing of cereals, beans, potatoes and oilseed rape, and, by the 1950s, managed its own pedigree dairy herd. In 1952 it was also the backdrop to one of Britain's most gruesome double murders.

At that time the estate employed some forty workers, all responsible for various aspects of farm management. All were brought in because of their particular expertise, many being housed in the village itself, others in the surrounding areas. The estate office, which sat in the centre of the village opposite the Three Horse Shoes public house (today the Chequered Skipper), essentially managed the estate's-day to-day activities under farm manager John Dockraye. Almost all the estate workers, therefore, had easy access to him and the estate office. The exception was George Peach and his wife, Lillian. They lived in what was known locally as West Lodge, a three-bedroom thatched, detached cottage which sat at the top end of the village's only through road. Their nearest neighbour was some 480 yards away. The cottage had been placed there by the Rothschilds as a gatehouse to manage access to the hamlet of Ashton Wold and the family mansion house. Isolated, surrounded on all sides by open fields and woodland, it was then, and still is today, a lonely and remote spot. Not that the Peaches had ever expressed any concern over the house's location.

Aged 64 and 67 respectively, George and Lillian had spent much of their life in rural, countryside locations, and this was the third house on the estate they had lived in. For George, employed as a gamekeeper and local handyman, the house was ideally placed for easy access onto the estate lands. Living just outside the village meant they were far enough away to maintain privacy, but near enough whenever George was needed to help with the cattle. In many ways they were the complete country couple, living simple, quiet lives and rarely leaving home. Certainly not wealthy, there was, however, a belief locally that they kept money hidden in the house. Speculation was no doubt driven by the Peach's life being outside the social circle of the village and what locals saw as a frugal lifestyle. Reclaiming and restoring their garden, which had been allowed to fall into disuse by previous occupants, was the greatest draw on their free time. George, in particular, was keen to grow his own seasonal food, as were many of the villagers, and had spent many of his weekends since moving in, back in 1948, trying to restore the patch of land beyond the back door. By the autumn of 1952 his time had been somewhat at a premium, what with the shorter days and an increased opportunity for overtime. Extra hours meant extra pay and George, who had been covering sick days and holidays throughout the year, was always a willing replacement. By October, he had taken on the role of cowman to assist herdsman John Oliver. Both men had worked together before, and whilst George may not have been expert in the rudiments of cattle management, John was. Happily, one compensated for the other and it was a partnership that worked well. Not that they generally worked in isolation. Head herdsman Francis Mahoney had been brought to the estate from Hereford in July that year because of his experience and expertise. Colonel Lane, who ran the estate alongside his wife, the Honourable Miriam Lane (Lord Rothschild's sister), was proud of their cattle, had won prizes and prestige through showing them and was intent on improving that success. Mahoney was a valuable addition to the team. For the Ashton estate, October's big event was the Dairy Show held at Olympia in London.

By Friday, 24 October 1952, Mahoney and the fourth member of the dairy team, Fred Hadman, had been in London for ten days, leaving George and John Oliver working alone out of Mill Farm. Standing at the southern edge of the village, the farm was being used that Friday to house one of the dairy cows that was having difficulty calving. Neither of the men wanted to call in a vet, so had shared the responsibility of monitoring the mother's progress throughout the morning. At 12.30 pm, with no sign of a birth, George decided to cycle back to West Lodge for lunch, leaving John Oliver to cope alone. He stayed away for two hours. Oliver later claimed he had never asked why, but believed, because it was so unusual for George to have done that, something had happened at home. The two men then worked together for the next three hours. Farm manager John Dockraye brought their weekly pay later in the afternoon, asked George to help with the milking next day and, with the cow still in calf, George left for home at around 6.00 pm. Before he left, he arranged with John Oliver for someone to come and fetch him from home during the night if needed to help with the birth if the cow was still in difficulties. That was the last time anyone saw him alive.

At 9.55 am the following morning (Saturday, 25 October), butcher's roundsman Laurence Wright began his morning round delivering meat to various customers in Ashton village. He had a late start that morning, delayed by a visit to the dentist – he had suffered overnight with a sore mouth after having some teeth removed the previous day – so was behind schedule when he arrived at West Lodge with the Sunday joint. Wright was surprised to find no-one at home after knocking on the back door, particularly Mrs Peach, who would normally be busy in the kitchen at that time on a Saturday. General practice for people at the time was to leave a plate just inside the lavatory door, which was accessible from the outside, if they were likely to be out when he called. The meat was well wrapped and never likely to be left out for long. But on this occasion there was no plate, so he carried the meat back to his van. He then noticed the window into the coal bunker was open, which in itself was not unusual; what was unusual was all the window curtains still being closed. Something, Wright suddenly realised, was wrong in the Peach house.

He made a quick drive back to the Three Horse Shoes pub and told the landlord, Frank Slater, what he had found. Slater in turn decided they needed to inform the estate's farm office, and the two of them walked over to inform John Dockraye. The latter already knew George Peach had not turned up at Mill Farm earlier that morning, after John Oliver had reported his absence some hours earlier, but had simply presumed illness. Still not overly concerned, Dockraye told his secretary to drive up to the lodge and see what was wrong. Slater offered his support and went with her.

When they arrived at the lodge, Slater went in alone through the front door, which was unlocked. Inside, the house was dark. He called out a couple of times, and after receiving no response he ran upstairs. At the top of those stairs was a short, narrow landing. There were three bedrooms. To his immediate left was a door to the back bedroom, which was closed and locked; a door directly in front of him, slightly ajar, led to the bedroom at the side of the house; to his right, a door, closed, gave access to the bedroom at the front of the house. Slater chose the middle bedroom and pushed the door open. Lillian Peach lay on the bed, breathing heavily, her face, throat and neck covered in blood. The bedclothes had been pulled back down to her feet, which remained covered. She was unable to speak. Realizing she was beyond any help that his rudimentary First Aid skills could offer, he wasted no time in getting back to the office. Once there, he alerted Dockraye to the seriousness of the situation, telling him he thought she had cut her throat. Whilst he tried to explain in greater detail just what he had seen, the estate's chauffeur, Albert Christopher, who had arrived at the office minutes earlier, suggested they go back and try to help. Dockraye was left to organize an ambulance and get police to the scene whilst the two men returned to the lodge.

In Christopher's statement to police, he said that when he arrived at the house, which was in darkness, he looked into the downstairs rooms: 'I saw that the pantry door was open, the curtains were all drawn, and we switched the lights on. Seeing nothing downstairs I went upstairs with Mr Slater.'

Once upstairs, he pulled the bedclothes back up and across Lillian Peach, then went out onto the landing with Slater to try to gain entry to the locked bedroom. It took some considerable effort, but brute force eventually forced the door. George Peach lay in bed, as if asleep, but when they switched on the light they could see he had been battered about the head, blood streaking the wall behind the bed head and the ceiling above. Cold to the touch and clearly dead, there was little to be done, so they went back outside to await help.

Oundle GP Ivor Spurrel arrived minutes later. In his later statement to police, he explained how he had tried to help Lillian Peach, but that her injuries were so severe there was little that could have been done without blood transfusions and expert resuscitation. He eventually wrapped her in blankets to make moving her easier for the ambulance when it arrived. In the case of George Peach, he made a cursory examination but left the body in situ: 'I went quickly to a back bedroom where I found the body of Mr Peach lying in a single bed. He was obviously dead and probably had been so for 4 or 5 hours or more judging by the advanced stage of rigor mortise and the fact that his body, even under the bedclothes, was cold.'

At that stage the ambulance and police arrived, which cut short his examination, and he gave what assistance he could to facilitate the removal of Lillian Peach from her bed. The ambulance then took her off to hospital in Peterborough. As they left, he returned upstairs, along with Inspector

Harold Peel of the police, to resume his examination of the body in the back bedroom:

> 'He was lying tucked up tidily in his bed with no obvious suggestion of struggle indicated. His head was lying on its left side on the pillow which was blood soaked. There was a deep gash over his left temple and over the left lower jaw extending down into the neck. These wounds suggested that they had been effected by a semi-sharp instrument such as a blunt axe.'

He went on to state that there was a trail of dried blood leading from one side of the bed out onto the landing and into the bedroom of Mrs Peach, and that the key to George Peach's bedroom door, which had been locked, had not been found.

Inspector Peel, the first senior policeman on the scene, made a preliminary examination of the house after the doctor had left. According to his later statement, nothing was out of place. The back door was locked, with the key being left inside the lock on the inside. The pantry door was open, a small window giving access to that room was also open and a small pane of glass had apparently been removed. On the table inside the kitchen was a key to a mortice lock, presumably the front door. He reported that nothing else appeared out of place: 'The house appeared to be as normal as anyone would leave it. There were no signs of a search having been made and I looked into the pantry and saw that the window was open and was not fastened on the ratchet arm.'

The upstairs rooms also showed no signs that a search had been made of any of the bedrooms, and police initially believed nothing had been stolen. However, they did believe entry was gained via that pantry window. Crime scene photographs in the police files do not add any credibility to that belief. The pantry was packed with crockery, saucepans and other kitchen paraphernalia, which would have made access extremely difficult. The window itself was very narrow, and the wide internal sill still cluttered with no signs of disturbance. Nevertheless, in the eyes of local police, this was a burglary gone wrong, and that was the direction the investigation was to follow from the moment Inspector Peel made his report.

It was also a crime that the police felt ill-equipped to investigate. Murder in rural Northamptonshire was rare, so rare in fact that by 2.00 pm that day they decided to call in Scotland Yard, the belief being that they had the expertise and the necessary support to handle what locally they believed would be a complex investigation. As things turned out, they were very wrong. When Inspector Wilfred Tarr and Detective Sergeant Albert Foster arrived at Oundle railway station from London late that night, thoughts of failure were never contemplated. Perhaps they should have been. The inspector had been in Hereford for a large part of the year, investigating the murder of shopkeeper Maria Hill, and he had not solved that crime. Perhaps the idea in 1952 that Scotland Yard officers were better at solving murder outside the capital than police local to the crime scene was flawed. However, sixty-odd years ago that was not accepted thinking and not likely to have been seriously considered at a senior level.

The two London detectives set themselves up in Oundle and held a meeting with the investigating officers that same night. Being told upon arrival that Lillian Peach had died without regaining consciousness obviously complicated matters. Double murder tended to muddy the waters somewhat. A burglar committing one murder during a failed robbery is one thing; murdering both householders must surely have thrown this motive into question. Inspector Tarr did tend, however, publicly at least, to support the notion of robbery gone wrong. I think it fair to say he had an open mind and was prepared to look into other possible motives for the killings. Whatever those thoughts may have been, he never shared them with the press, happy enough for them to continue reporting with a bias slant supporting the burglary theory.

The first avenue for the investigating team to explore was the obvious one: family. The Peaches had a son, Jack. He lived away in Staines, where he worked as an engineer. He had already been located by the time of Scotland Yard's arrival, and the London police had brought him to Ashton just after midnight. Obviously, Jack knew the village and the surrounding areas extremely well. Educated in Oundle, he had moved away after his marriage in 1947, but maintained a regular family contact. Joan, his wife, along with his daughter, both moved back to Ashton to live with his parents on a full-time basis from 1950 until May 1952, whilst he sorted out work and a place to live permanently in London. For the police, therefore, Jack and his family were vital in understanding how the Peach household functioned on a daily basis, the friends they kept, their relationships with the rest of the village and the personal belongings they owned.

From meetings they had with Jack over the next couple of days, they quickly identified that George Peach's wages, £9 and 13 shillings paid on the Friday afternoon (24 October), were missing. So was any money retained by Lillian Peach. It was George's habit to keep a few shillings for himself, the rest of the money she kept in a handbag in an upstairs bedroom, paying household bills from it as well as using it to buy food. The handbag had been found, but no purse or money, which obviously lent credence to the robbery motive that police were following. The second avenue, and in support of the burglary theory, was opportunist theft. If someone had climbed in through that pantry window, as local police had been quick to accept, it was likely to have been a stranger. Locking doors in Ashton was not common practice. Peach had even left the front door to the house open. Besides, as perhaps Jack Peach was able to show, there was no need to steal from each other. Anything needed could easily be borrowed; everyone knew each other, and while there may have been the occasional friction, there was never really a need to burgle a neighbour. However, not far away from the village stood Polebrook camp. Built for the RAF on Rothschild estate land at the start of the war, it had been the home of the US Air Force up until the war ended when its primary use came to an end.

In 1952 it was used, in part, to house itinerant and immigrant labour, essentially a mix of Ukrainian, Polish, Scottish and English labourers. All men paid seven shillings and sixpence each week for accommodation in the hostel there, the money deducted from any pay they received. Food was also available to buy in the onsite canteen if they wished. Possessing a variety of skills, most were employed at the nearby Molesworth Aerodrome. A bus arrived every morning to take them off to work, returning each evening around 5.30 pm. It was a workforce that fitted the police profile; strangers to the area, unfamiliar with the locals, their traditions or working practices, but surrounded by homes that had what they were struggling to earn: money. On Sunday, 26 October, police arrived at the hostel looking for any of the thirty-six-strong workforce who had been absent from the camp on the Friday night of George and Lillian Peach's murder. It took no time at all for them to locate Nikolaus Skoropei.

At Polebrook, sleeping in the hostel meant sharing a room. Some rooms were made up of four residents sleeping together, others only two. In Skoropei's case, he shared with fellow Ukrainian Alfred Nimero, which meant his movements were always known. On Friday, 24 October, according to Nimero, Skoropei had borrowed a bicycle and left the camp around 6.30 pm and did not return until around 6.00 am the following morning. No-one else was found to have been absent during the crucial hours, which made the Ukrainian the first key suspect in the police investigation. He was brought in to Oundle for questioning twenty-four hours later, his inability to account for his movements during the early hours of Saturday morning simply adding to a growing level of suspicion.

According to his statement, he had gone to a dance at the Drill Hall in Oundle. There he had stayed until 1.00 am. He was able to describe or give names to the people he met, danced with or bought drinks for, but he was not able to explain just why it had taken him some five hours to cycle home along the Oundle to Polebrook road, a distance of around 5 miles on a road that was a relatively straight. He claimed too much beer had made the journey difficult, and somewhere along the route he had fallen over and fallen asleep. That was not impossible, but the weather that night had been cold, with a strong wind blowing, not very conducive to sleeping outdoors. Understandably, the police had doubts. They also knew that along that same road lay the narrow road entrance into Ashton village. Consequently, they wasted no time in seizing his belongings, and in particular all his clothes, which were sent off for forensic analysis.

By the time his interview took place, they had already received the post-mortem report on George and Lillian Peach and knew all too well just how damaging the attacks on them had been, and more importantly just how much blood had been sprayed around the bedrooms and inevitably onto the killer. According to the report on the autopsy performed by James Webster, professor of forensic medicine and toxicology at Birmingham, George had been struck no more than six times, all the blows struck to the head whilst he slept. In the professor's opinion, he never woke up, never saw his killer and all the blows had been struck from the left side of the bed, which lay against the back wall facing the door. By using body temperature, amount of urine in the bladder and the condition of gastric digestion, Professor Webster was further able to place time of death as being around 2.00 am.

In the case of Lillian, he found the attack had been far more severe. She had also been awake when first attacked, and had fought hard for her life. Defensive injuries evident on both hands showed she had been struck from both the right and the left sides. She suffered in all some thirty-one blows to her head, all caused, as in the case of her husband, by a hammer of some type, but a hammer that was also able to inflict stab wounds in places. Professor Webster reported:

> 'It is perfectly obvious from her body and Peach's body that the majority of the wounds were caused by a hammer type of instrument, but this stab wound clearly indicates that there was some sort of spike or similar arrangement on the other side of the hammer, and from Peach's body I would favour the use of such instrument as a tiler's hammer or type of hammer used by bricklayers in tapping home bricks … The degree of violence … would indicate that you

have either a person of extraordinarily well-developed physic or a person of moderate physic wielding a heavy weapon.'

The other odd fact raised by his report was that some wounds exhibited a Y-shape mark, which could have suggested a claw hammer. The report provided the police with a somewhat confused picture, but one that strongly suggested the killer would have received significant blood splatter on his clothes and could possibly have used a coal hammer. The Peach's coal bunker window, as reported by the butcher's roundsman, had been found open, but with no coal hammer inside. Police believed the possession of such a hammer to be common to all households in the village, and also that if the professor was correct in his assessment of the attacker's stature, then it was hardly likely he broke in through the pantry window. It seemed at that point that Skoropei did not fit the profile.

This report was a lifeline for Skoropei, and then when the forensic analysis of his clothes eventually arrived on Inspector Tarr's desk, whilst it revealed some odd spots of blood, there was nothing of any real significance. The Ukrainian slowly slipped from the police radar, and the enquiry turned back toward the village and those living in it.

From the outset there had been a belief amongst the estate's workforce that the murder had been committed closer to home. Rumour speculated that Peach had known something about the mechanics of the farm management used on the estate; something about how the cattle were overseen, recorded and maintained. He had talked about it, expressed an angry opinion and had threatened to expose some sort of fraudulent activity to Miriam Lane, a woman in whom he had great trust. Various employees, some anonymously, talked or wrote to the police to alert them to this fact, pointing at this as being reason enough to see him dead. Families, homes, jobs and reputations rested on his being silenced, or so the argument ran.

Whether the information was accepted by the Scotland Yard detectives as a valid motive for murder is not known. They certainly treated it with some caution, and understandably so – gossip can be dangerous in a murder enquiry – but they also knew it could hold a truth as yet uncovered. At the end of the first week of the investigation, they organized a house-to-house search of the village. Finding the hammer used in the murders was crucial. Fingers had, by this time, been pointed at one or two individuals, so its discovery became vital. The general thinking was that if the killer lived locally, he would possibly have kept the hammer rather than discard it. But the intention to search had been well advertised. On 1 November, as the house-to-house search began, Florence Marsh, who lived at the Chapel Farm house in the centre of the village, made an accidental but timely discovery: lying on top of fallen leaves in her garden was a claw hammer.

Forensic examination subsequently found blood and human hair stuck to the hammer head, which careful analysis proved to have come from the head of George Peach. The blood group, type A, also matched. The murder weapon had been found, though it still left unanswered questions. It was not a spiked coal hammer, which is what police had begun the search to find and which had been thought to have caused some of the wounds. It had also been found on top of leaves, not under them, as would have been expected in the middle of autumn several days after the murders. Nevertheless, it was a breakthrough. The garden in which it was found lay some 600 yards away from West Lodge. It had a boundary wall that ran alongside the only road through Ashton, and strongly suggested the killer had discarded it as he walked back through the village after the murders.

Four days later, Jack Peach confirmed that his father's watch was missing, possibly taken by the killer before he left the house. Whilst enquiries continued in Ashton, the police investigation also moved to Molesworth Airfield, home to US Air Force at the time and the place of work for many who lived at the Polebrook hostel. It was really no more than a process of elimination. Nothing of any significance was found, the search merely part of an all-embracing investigation that, by this time, had successfully accounted for virtually all traffic movement around eastern Northamptonshire on the night of the killings. Even passengers who boarded trains at Peterborough railway station were traced, it being the nearest operating station that night. Back in the village, police resumed their examination of coal bunkers, a second hammer clearly not ruled out at that point. They also took statements from the men George Peach had worked with, and asked the Peaches' coal deliverymen to try to identify the claw hammer. Whilst this valuable investigative work helped move the enquiry forward, it did little to help solve the mystery of the double killing.

All that was known for certain was that on the night of the murders, the only confirmed movement in and around Ashton village in the early hours of 25 October was made by Frederick Hadman and Francis Mahoney, who had arrived back in Ashton after the Olympia show. Hadman confirmed he unloaded the cattle and met Mahoney at around 12.45 am at Chapel Farm, near the centre of the village. The men had held a brief conversation and then gone home to their respective beds. The murder itself had been accepted as having taken place at 2.00 am, with a claw hammer used in the killing discovered in a garden. Everything else was pure speculation, including the growing belief the killing had been intentional. The 'robbery gone wrong theory', certainly amongst some police officers, had lost its credibility as a viable motive.

For the next few days, no further progress was made and the investigation faltered. Then on 13 November came a sudden and unexpected break-through. At 3.50 pm, PC Gibson and Detective Constable Etats were sent out to search the hedgerows and grass verges in the village, and discovered a woman's purse. It lay hidden on the left-hand side of the road, some 800 yards (731m) away from West Lodge at the entrance to the garden of farm manager John Dockraye. Its position at the end of the village, where the narrow road bends to join the road to neighbouring Polebrook village, tended to suggest the route taken by the killer after the murder. Forensic examination of the purse, which contained a threepenny piece, found that mould had formed in places on the leather, indicating it had lain undisturbed for several days. The Scotland Yard detectives wasted no time in confirming the ownership. Enough locals had seen Lillian Peach use it to know it had belonged to her. Though not all agreed, some thought perhaps there was a second purse. But as far as the investigation was concerned, there was no supporting evidence for that theory and so it was not pursued further.

Nikolaus Skoropei was briefly back in the picture. The position of the purse when found, and its location in relation to the road's access to Polebrook and the work camp, were perhaps seen as a clearer indication of his possible involvement. Inspector Tarr, concerned that Skoropei could have been eliminated from enquiries too early, had him questioned a second time. But, just as before, nothing new came from the interview. Skoropei had little to add to his initial statement, and the Scotland Yard detective had no supporting evidence to disprove it. He was released the same day.

By the end of November, no other leads had been found. Francis Mahoney, head herdsman, had reported finding a coal hammer in his car, which he had handed in to police. A second hammer was reported seen inside his coal shed, but he denied ownership. Perhaps it was a village conspiracy to point an accusing finger in his direction. But it had no substance, and Mahoney left Ashton before the year was out. No one else was ever arrested or brought in for questioning, and the Yard's detectives were back in London by the start of 1953.

So who killed George and Lillian Peach? The mystery has endured for almost seventy years, and will probably do so for all time now. It seems clear from police files that the villagers believed the killer was one of their own. Names were mentioned, and neighbours inculpated. The notion of a burglary gone wrong was never accepted by them, nor, I would guess, by the police. The common belief was, and still is, that George Peach uncovered something illegal being practised in relation to the handling and management of the cattle held by the estate. Exactly what that was has never really been discussed or confirmed openly, but seems to be the accepted opinion by most people looking at this crime. The trail of clues – the claw hammer and the purse – a bit like a paper trail, would appear to have been placed long after the deed had been done. The hammer being found on top of leaves, not underneath, in the middle of autumn after strong winds and the start of a house-to-house search, is perhaps an indicator of a home-grown killer. It could also suggest that once Skoropei was brought in for questioning, that same killer discarded the hammer along with the purse to suggest a route home that only the killer would have taken had he been living in the hostel outside Polebrook village. Or is that a little too contrived? Either way, the post-mortem suggests a possible second weapon, and the killer, or killers, had to have been blood-spattered. The killing of Lillian Peach was savage beyond belief. Anyone involved in that attack was not going to walk away free of bloodstaining, which strongly suggests a killer or killers living close by who could change their clothes quickly and unseen.

My own theory is that George Peach was the intended target that night. Whoever entered West Lodge at 2.00 am went in by the front door and knew the sleeping arrangements of the house – the fact that George slept in the back bedroom – and attacked him first, then carefully locked his body in his room and took away the key. I believe this was done because they did not want his wife to discover his body until the next morning. But it all went wrong when she heard his door close and called out. At that point there had to have been a choice for the killer: run and hope Lillian did not get out of bed in time to identify them, or kill her. He, or they, chose to kill, possibly because they heard her trying to get out of bed. Maybe she had put a light on, her bedroom door was open, there was insufficient time to escape before being seen or she had recognized something, a voice, a movement or an individual. We will never know for certain. What we do know is that the inside of the house the following morning did not reflect with any real accuracy just how it had looked in the early hours of the morning when the murders were committed. Too many people had been in and out before the police arrived; things had been moved, doors had been opened or closed, which was understandable once it had been established that Mrs Peach was still alive. All these years later, therefore, the murders are still unsolved, with very little chance of that status ever being changed.

## Chapter 13

# The Freezer Murder

*The murder of Anne Noblett, 1957*

On 31 January 1958, after a search that had lasted for the whole of that month, the body of 17-year-old Anne Noblett was discovered in scrubland in Rose Grove Woods, known locally as Young's Wood, near Horn Hill, Whitwell, some 6 miles south of Hitchin in Hertfordshire. The discovery, which was quite accidental, was made by brothers Hugh and Brian Symonds, who were out walking their dog on land they knew well. Essentially it was a game reserve, well used by dog walkers and regularly patrolled by local gamekeepers.

Anne's body lay fully clothed, on her back, her arms folded neatly across her chest. She was still wearing her spectacles and her shoes, which were clean despite the surrounding ground being muddy. She wore a winter coat, which was understandably wet, but the clothes beneath were dry. Bizarrely, scattered over her and around where she lay were a number of coins; purposely placed there, it is believed, to show she had not been murdered in the course of a robbery. Murder in commission of a felony was a capital offence and meant her killer would face the death penalty if caught. According to the police, who examined her body in situ, she was also extremely cold; so cold in fact that she must have been in some sort of refrigerated state before being brought to the wood. It meant she had probably been placed in a freezer of some sort for some time prior to her discovery.

That one fact, along with the location, initially caused police the greatest area of concern. Rose Grove Woods were not easily accessible by car, and the area of scrubland where the body was placed meant it must have been carried some 300 yards (274m) from the nearest vehicular access point and 75 yards (68m) inside the wood. Not only that, but Anne Noblett weighed some 11 stone (69.8kg), which is significant in itself, but if she had also been in some sort of frozen state when brought to the site, as police suspected, then the physical effort needed to carry the body would have been considerable. The likelihood of that being done by one man was virtually impossible, which led Detective Superintendent Richard Lewis, leading the team from Scotland Yard, to surmise that if that was the case then there had to have been a second party involved.

It took a week before Home Office pathologist Doctor Francis Camps was able to throw more light on just how Anne's body had been preserved and its impact on the crime scene. According to his post-mortem results, presented at the inquest on 10 February 1958, the body had probably not been in a deep freeze for a lengthy period of time, nor had she been in a rigid state when carried to the place where her body was found. Rather, she had been placed in refrigeration for a short period almost immediately after death. That would obviously lower her body temperature significantly, and in turn would slow decay and ensure preservation for a much longer period than could otherwise have been expected. Possibly it was done to confuse or disguise the time of her death and hinder the inevitable police investigation that would follow the body's discovery. But what that process had not accomplished was to hide the fact that Anne had eaten before her death and that food had been retained in her stomach, allowing the time of death to be placed shortly after the time of her known disappearance. Nor did it hide the fact she had been sexually assaulted and asphyxiated by some means. In other words, the whole operation failed in its attempt at obfuscation. However, the chilling process had been successful in ensuring there were no visible clues on her body indicating who her attacker could have been, which for the killer was perhaps all that really mattered. She had also been refrigerated in a naked state and re-dressed afterwards. Buttons on her clothing were incorrectly fastened, a clear indicator that her clothes had been removed. They were also dry, which suggests they had been kept separate from her body for some time before being replaced.

From that point on, police began talking to farmers with refrigeration equipment. They also brought in various refrigeration experts to examine the possibility that Anne's body could have been kept at low temperatures without resorting to actual mechanical refrigeration, such as being packed in ice. How successful they were is not known, but it did change initial police thinking on just how difficult, or not, it would have been to move her body. A very cold but not frozen corpse made transportation easier in many ways. It did not remove entirely the notion that two men carried out the placing of her body, but did allow for the possibility that it could also, with effort, have been carried out by a lone killer.

From the outset, police believed Anne Noblett had probably known her attacker; whether personally or as a passing acquaintance is obviously conjecture. But on the evening of 30 December 1957, Anne, after attending a dance class in Harpenden, had boarded a Green Line bus home. The driver dropped her outside the Cherry Tree pub on Marshalls Heath Lane at Wheathampstead, which was unlit, at around 6.00 pm. At that point she was only 400 yards (366m) from home. Shirley Edwards, who knew Anne, saw her at that time walking away from the bus stop on her way to the family's house. To disappear so quickly meant someone, probably in a car, had stopped to offer a lift, and that someone she probably knew. In 1957, unlike today, cars were still not so common on many British roads; most households did not own one or have expectations that they ever would. It is a realistic supposition to believe the police were right about this. Why would you get into a car with a driver you did not know when you lived nearby?

Anne had been away from Wheathampstead for the previous four years being educated at the Chatelard School in Montreux, Switzerland, a boarding school for young girls near to Chateau Du Chatelard where she had mixed with girls from around the world, although most were British, and returned home only for holidays. She had only been back in England since July and was probably making new friends and reacquainting herself with others, including adults, she was familiar with and no doubt trusted.

The search for her after her disappearance was widespread, and had started within hours of her not arriving home. Throughout the first week of January, some 300 people a day searched nearby fields, examined hedgerows and visited most open spaces in an attempt to find her. Since 6 January, police had created specialist three-man teams to search by-lanes, footpaths, ditches, outbuildings, haystacks and farms. Her father, Hugh Noblett, a poultry farmer and director of a business manufacturing protective headgear, helped to maintain a high profile with the press. Kidnapping was even considered as a possible motive for her disappearance at one point, but never seriously pursued. As the month progressed, so the search widened, with house-to-house enquiries and garden searches becoming a daily event, progress followed closely by both local and national press as police moved from district to district.

Conceivably it was this single factor that forced the killer to place Anne's body in Rose Grove Woods. By the time of her discovery, police searches had covered a vast area. There can be little doubt that the killer, having decided to hold on to the body, had a sudden and serious need to be rid of it. What police needed to ascertain once the crime scene had been uncovered was just how long the body had lain there. Scotland Yard brought in botanists from the Rothamsted Agricultural Experimental Station, one of the oldest agricultural research institutions in the world. Located in Harpenden, it was their task to investigate the ground beneath which Anne Noblett's body had been found. Unlike other outdoor murder scenes, due to the cold state of the body, its overall lack of decomposition and the fact that it was January; there was no significant staining of the ground or clear depression of the undergrowth. According to local gamekeepers, it was also a patch of open ground regularly patrolled, though just how regularly never appears to have been clearly confirmed. Nevertheless, I have no doubt that police were made aware that decay would normally begin once the body temperature had fallen to around 10C (50F). In Anne's case, it appears that had not happened. Therefore, it was extremely sensible to request experts to examine the ground she had lain on in an attempt to tie down a specific time period during which her killer could have brought her there. As far as I can determine, their results suggested that the killer had placed her in the clearing around two weeks prior to the Symonds brother stumbling across her. That meant around 17 January, which definitely gave credibility to the idea it had been the house searches that had forced his hand.

Whilst all this was ongoing, as if they did not have enough to deal with over the appalling death of their daughter, the Noblett family were receiving anonymous phone calls. They were malicious more than threatening, and the police were sure they had nothing to do with Anne's murder. However, it was something they could certainly do without, and the murder team resolved to find the caller, which they eventually did. Twenty-five-year-old Walter Nunn was caught as he left a public call box. He had made thirty calls to the Noblett house, all intended for Anne's mother, Ida. He appeared in court in March 1958 and was sent to prison for six months.

By this time, sadly, the murder investigation was being scaled down from the heights it had reached in February, as no clues had been unearthed and no significant arrests made. The case was no longer deemed newsworthy, and with the Scotland Yard detectives back in London it fell out of favour with the British press. Then, in June 1958, a spark of interest suddenly flared as it became known that police officers had been alerted by Belgian police that a man Scotland Yard had sought earlier in the year had been found in Belgium. Albert Braeckman, a refrigeration engineer, surrendered himself to Belgian police after newspapers there had carried details of his name in relation to the murder at Wheathampstead. He was interviewed on 13 June for over five hours, but it came to nothing and the case fell from public view again.

It was revisited a second time in January 1960 when the *Birmingham Post* received an anonymous call from a man claiming to have murdered Anne Noblett, and also 29-year-old Stephanie Baird in a room at Birmingham's YMCA. Stephanie's murder was a particularly savage and bloody affair, for which a man named Patrick Byrne was arrested later that same month. Scottish serial killer Peter Manuel was also considered a possible suspect in Stephanie's murder. He had been executed in Glasgow in July 1958 for the murder of six people, and had thought to have been involved in others, including some murders in England.

There have been other links too. The 1958 murder of Dutch girl Mary Kriek was perhaps the most plausible. She was discovered battered to death in a ditch at Boxstead, near Colchester, after alighting from a bus. There are clear similarities between the crimes, and police investigating both killings appeared to work closely together for a time during the first half of 1958. There was support, at least for a while, for the theory that one killer could have murdered both young women. However, their combined efforts came to nothing and no-one was ever apprehended, which has left both cases still unsolved today.

# Index